AF576855

Major funding for the Israel/North Carolina Cultural Exchange has been provided by the North Carolina Department of Cultural Resources and the State of Israel.

MAJOR CONTRIBUTORS TO THE ISRAEL/NORTH CAROLINA CULTURAL EXCHANGE

State of North Carolina, Department of Cultural Resources
State of Israel, Ministry of Foreign Affairs

The Mary Duke Biddle Foundation
The Blumenthal Foundation
Carolina Power & Light Company
The Kaplan Family Foundation
NationsBank
The Wachovia Foundation, Inc.

Anna Lou Cassell
Mr. and Mrs. Benjamin Cone, Jr.
Bernard Gutterman

The Adelman Family Fund
Richard D. Adelman
Mr. and Mrs. Arthur Bluethenthal
Robert C. Cone
Jean B. Falk
Sara Frooman
Ronald and Susan Green
Greensboro Jewish Federation
Arthur Gordon
Mary Gut
Mr. and Mrs. R. Philip Hanes, Jr.
Robert S. Kadis
Mr. and Mrs. Robert J. Lee
Henry Samuel Levinson
Anne Cone Liptzin
Dr. and Mrs. Myron B. Liptzin
Mazel Tov Gifts
Mr. and Mrs. Paul J. Michaels
Kay and Dave Phillips Foundation
Mr. and Mrs. Marshall Rauch
Stanley Robboy
Susan Rosenthal
Mr. and Mrs. Norman G. Samet
Dr. and Mrs. Paul Sarazen
Daniel Satisky
Leah Louise B. Tannenbaum
Mr. and Mrs. Smedes York

Denis I. and Patricia Ann Becker
Ruth Beesch
Mr. and Mrs. Frank Brenner
William L. Cassell
Thomas L. Chatham
Evan and Larkin Coffey
Barbara and Harvey Colchamiro
The Dover Foundation, Inc.
Mr. and Mrs. Stanley H. Fox
Bluma K. Greenberg
Mr. and Mrs. Howard Guld
Dr. and Mrs. Soloman P. Hersh
Mr. and Mrs. Daniel Horvitz
Abram Kanof
Dolph and Naomi Klein
Cary & Susie Kosten
Ruth Leder
Mr. and Mrs. Ross Levin
Stuart J. Levin
J.H.M. Meyer
Ruth Mary Meyer
Betty P. Reigot
Mr. and Mrs. Arnold Shertz
Gloria Silber
Robert Sosnik
Ann Lewallen Spencer
Charles M. and Shirley F. Weiss
Tex Williams
Mr. and Mrs. Edward O. Woolner

Curator: Nella Cassouto

L O N G M E M O R Y | **SHORT MEMORY**

Preface and Acknowledgements

It gives me great pleasure to welcome audiences to an art experience of profound depth. As part of the Israel/North Carolina Cultural Exchange, City Gallery of Contemporary Art is privileged to present recent works by ten Israeli artists in an exhibition titled "Long Memory/Short Memory".

American perceptions of the Middle East are predominantly shaped by the terrorist reports that routinely occupy media accounts. Thankfully, North Carolina's leadership felt its citizens needed a more in-depth understanding of Israel's culture and the people who occupy our fascination. Educational exposure to the cultural heritage of the Israelis will contribute to North Carolina's comprehension and valuation of both recent and historical events in that land. City Gallery of Contemporary Art is grateful that our two governments have generously shared in bringing this experience to Raleigh.

City Gallery's marvelous exhibition would not be in Raleigh without the insight and vision of our very forward thinking Governor James B. Hunt, Jr. and former Israeli Prime Minister Shimon Peres, and the passion and stewardship of North Carolina Secretary of Cultural Resources Betty Ray McCain and Deputy Secretary Elizabeth F. Buford. Uri Bar Ner, Deputy Director General of the Ministry of Foreign Affairs for Culture and Science; and Arye Mekel, Consul General of Israel to the Southeastern United States, have been generous friends and supporters of the exchange from its beginnings in 1994. Major funding for the cultural exchange has been provided by the State of North Carolina through the Department of Cultural Resources and the Ministry of Foreign Affairs of the State of Israel. The educational programs surrounding "Long Memory/Short Memory" have been funded by the City of Raleigh Arts Commission.

John Coffey of the North Carolina Museum of Art also deserves much praise. He is our state's expert on contemporary Israeli art and previously curated a beautiful show of Moshe Kupferman's work. By inviting a group of museum directors and curators from around the Triangle to the North Carolina Museum of Art to discuss the possibility of collaboration between our institutions and Israel, did he realize what he would create? The idea took off with much enthusiasm as John challenged our assumptions and thinking about Israeli art. He supported our ideas and helped us grow as curators. (John is held in such high esteem in Israel that one is treated as a long-time friend by merely mentioning his name there.) John Coffey deserves enormous thanks for bringing us all together and for overseeing this project.

Also deserving of thanks and praise is Nella Cassouto, a wonderful curator, whom I met on my first visit to Israel. My intention for City Gallery's project was to have a strong collaboration between our American exhibition space and its audiences and each of the Israeli artists. Nella's knowledge of the contemporary Israeli art scene was seen as pivotal in our efforts to make this happen, and we immediately asked her to be a member of our team. Tom Spleth, City Gallery's curator for the exhibition, and Nella combined forces in the creation of an exhibition that presents their joint vision. I commend both for their earnest desire to work together and to present "Long Memory/Short Memory" to City Gallery's audiences.

Numerous City Gallery staff members participated in the realization of this project as well. Sincere thanks to Colette Waters, Curator of Education; Julia Waterfall, Development Officer; Joey Howard, Administrative Assistant/Preparator; Greg Flynn, Gallery Attendant; and David Simonton, Photographer and Gallery Attendant. Special thanks are also due to Diane Pettus, who edited the text for City Gallery; to the Hebrew editor and translator, Hana Stern; and to Malka Jagendorf, for her English translation and editing of the Hebrew text.

In conclusion, and on a personal level, I want to express the pride and gratitude I feel as one who was born and educated in North Carolina. This is a state that has provided its citizens with a world class museum of art and the nation's first arts council and school of the arts. Few states have considered educating their public in such a progressive way. It seems natural that North Carolina has once again taken the lead in teaching us, its citizens, through the arts, this time choosing as the educational objective public awareness and understanding of the arts of Israel and their cultural impact on the world. City Gallery of Contemporary Art, and I as its director, are extremely honored to be a part of this dialogue.

Denise Dickens

Director

I would like to thank Denise Dickens and Tom Spleth, who have made this international venture an adventure. My thanks too to Dr. Gannit Ankori for calling my attention to Toni Morrison's ***The Site of Memory.*** I am deeply grateful to my family - my sons Shmulik, Yaron, and Dror, and my sister, Ada Burko - for their loving encouragement; and to Moshe Kron for his steadfast help and support.

I am most indebted to John Coffey, whose dynamism and interest in Israeli art was the springboard for the initiative that made this exhibition possible.

Nella Cassouto

Long Memory / Short Memory

Nella Cassouto

Only because of forgetfulness
Our lives are lives
And they are lives
Only because of memory.
T. Carmi

Memory is an understanding of the past, a process of maturation in which we preserve material and add to it elements that change its meaning. As we evolve throughout our lives, our perception of the past changes accordingly.

For me, a considerable part of memory is connected with personal pain and sorrow, which over time have become part of daily existence. The filtering process activated by memory is what enables the reprocessing of the actuality and the revealing of viewpoints and possibilities that I had not discerned before. That is how the idea was born to mount an exhibition where each work would be chosen on the basis of its foundation on the basic motifs that stir the soul: memory, pain, sadness, forgetfulness, and fear - essentially, the components that create a work of art.

The ten artists participating in this exhibition represent what is happening in Israeli art today; their work embodies memory - of the Holocaust, of death, of war.

"Every Israeli artist is influenced by the weight of the Holocaust," artist Moshe Kupferman told me in January of 1990, adding: "Artists have grown up and matured charged with bearing that burden and

. . . the act of imagination is bound up with memory. You know, they straightened out the Mississippi River in places, to make room for houses and livable acreage. Occasionally the river floods these places. "Floods" is the word they use, but in fact it is not flooding; it is remembering. Remembering where it used to be. All water has a perfect memory and is forever trying to get back to where it was. Writers are like that: remembering where we were, what valley we ran through, what the banks were like, the light that was there and the route back to our original place. It is emotional memory - what the nerves and the skin remember as well as how it appeared. And a rush of imagination is our "flooding".
. . . Still, like water, I remember where I was before I was "straightened out".

The Site of Memory
Toni Morrison
Massachusetts-London 1990
p. 305

Will it ultimately reach the clear surface of my consciousness, this memory, this old, dead moment which the magnetism of an identical moment has travelled so far to importune, to disturb, to raise up out of the very depths of my being.
. . perhaps because of these memories, so long abandoned and put out of mind, nothing now survived, everything was scattered; the forms . . . were either obliterated or had been so long dormant as to have lost the power of expansion which would have allowed them to resume their place in my consciousness. But when from a long-distant past nothing subsists, after the people are dead, after the things are broken and scattered, still, alone, more fragile, but with more vitality, more unsubstantial, more persistent, more faithful, the smell and taste of things remain poised a long time, like souls, ready to remind us, waiting and hoping for their moment, amid the ruins of all the rest; and bear unfaltering, in the tiny and almost impalpable drop of their essence, the vast structure of recollection.

Swann's Way, Remembrance of Things Past
Marcel Proust
Trans. Scott Moncrieff
pp. 35-36

giving it expression." Kupferman's remarks seem to me to be connected with the act of remembering or, to put it differently, with the individual's mental power to evoke at a given moment something that happened to him in the past. Remembrance is the recalling of movements, skills, displays, words, ideas, that have been learned in the past. No less important is forgetfulness and its various causes, among them the unconscious repression from the conscious to the subconscious (oblivion), of experiences that are unpleasant to recall; yet traumatic experiences are not easily forgotten. In the course of maturation they tend to surface in a process of remembering and interpreting.

This exhibition gives expression to both the weight of the Holocaust and to the phenomenon of the existence of the Jewish people in a state of perennial threat of annihilation. There is no display of "images" that "represent the Holocaust," the "resistance movement," "the establishment of the State of Israel." The exhibition includes art works in which silence illuminates cognitively the sense of the past and the sense of the present, works that dredge crumbs of memory from the depths of the past and protect us from the possible onslaught of further trauma.

This story is drawing to a close and once more the question arises: have I succeeded in setting down even so much as a tiny part of what I wanted to express? As a matter of fact, this quest, this incessant confrontation with the past during these months, has become sufficient reason in itself, and a necessary undertaking. And the words of Gustav Meyrink leap to mind once more: "When knowledge comes, memory comes too, little by little . . ." - a sequence, however, that has been inverted here: when memory comes, knowledge comes too, little by little . . . " Knowledge and memory are one and the same thing."

. . . For the first time, it is true, we see a possibility of peace dawning, but nothing is certain. For the first time the end of the tunnel seems to be at hand, but there are those who consider the light glimpsed in the distance a dangerous mirage.
. . . But beyond these reflections on the immediate future, the uncertainty that now envelops us takes on another meaning and another dimension. It has always represented our manner of existence in the world, and in many respects, for better or worse, it has made us what we are. Sometimes when I think back on our history, not of these past few years, but rather its entire sweep, I can make out a perpetual movement back and forth, a search for roots, for normality and security, forever threatened down through the centuries, and I tell myself that the Jewish state may perhaps be only a step on the way of a people whose particular destiny has come to symbolize the endless quest - ever hesitant, ever begun anew - of all mankind.

When Memory Comes
Saul Friedlander
trans. Helen R. Lane
New York 1979, pp. 182-183

Like other native Israelis the only existence I know is shadowed by the perpetual threat of destruction, either in war or in long periods of attrition through constant tension and acts of terror. This reality became normative, natural, everyday - against the background of the Holocaust, the collective historical memory of every member of this society. Thus life in Israel is charged with what the writer David Grossman calls the unbearable lightness of death; because of the powerful presence of death, the danger of death and the fear of death, one sometimes senses in Israel a curious tendency to experience life as latent death ; a life that enables Israelis to explain their perceived mode of confrontation and acceptance of death as an integral part of life.

To all appearances, daily life goes on; cultural events take place, books are written, art is created, gardens are planted, shopping malls are opened. But in the chambers of the heart crouches the sadness that has become part of life for those who have been war-bereaved over the years.

Israeli society is centered on the child, the family, and friends - soul-mates and close companions who are like kin; each loss is

AUTOBIOGRAPHY

I died with the first blow and was buried
among the rocks of the field.
The raven taught my parents
what to do with me.

If my family is famous,
not a little of the credit goes to me.
My brother invented murder,
my parents invented grief,
I invented silence.

Afterwards the well-known events took place,
Our inventions were perfected. One thing led to another,
orders were given. There were those who murdered in their own way,
grieved in their own way.

I won't mention names
out of consideration for the reader,
since at first the details horrify
though finally they're a bore:

You can die once, twice, even seven times,
but you can't die a thousand times.
I can.
My underground cells reach everywhere.

When Cain began to multiply on the face of the earth,
I began to multiply in the belly of the earth,
and my strength has long been greater than his.
His legions desert him and go over to me,
and even this is only half a revenge.

Points of Departure
Dan Pagis
trans. Stephen Mitchell
1972, pp. 2-3

by all. Loss is not only personal in Israel. The fallen are mourned by the entire nation, as expressed in memorial days and in the contact that is maintained among bereaved families. Thus personal tragedy is commemorated in collective mourning.*

Through this exhibition I wish to relate to collective memory - of the past remembered not literally but figuratively, in images that change according to the needs of the society, either to create a myth, or in relation to the general perception of the images and mythology of the past, or parts of the past of different periods or cultures.

Society creates its own past through collective memory which is a recalling of the past not necessarily according to historical fact. A society's grasp of its past becomes a tool for art in the present, with its changing values. Ernest Renan has said: "Forgetfulness is a vital force in the creation of a nation, whose people share many things together, and forget many things together."

Apparently even the individuals in a society - and in our case, the artists - many of whom have never experienced personal loss, process the trauma, appropriating it for themselves, or revising it to

It was that special hour - I recognized it now, I recognized it here - my favorite hour in the camp, and a sharp, painful, futile desire grasped my heart: homesickness. All of a sudden everything came alive, everything came back, everything flooded my consciousness. I was surprised by strange moods, trembled at small memories. Yes, indeed, in a certain sense, life was purer, simpler back there. I remembered everything and everyone, even those who didn't interest me, but especially those whose existence I could validate by my presence here: Pjetyka, Bohus, the doctor, and all the rest of them.

I already begin to feel how readiness is growing, collecting inside me. I have to continue my uncontinuable life. My mother is waiting for me. She'll certainly be happy to see me, the poor dear. I recall how once she planned for me to become an engineer or a doctor or something like that. This is certainly what she wants. There is no impossibility that cannot be overcome (survived?), naturally, and further down the road, I now know, happiness lies in wait for me like an inevitable trap. Even back there, in the shadow of the chimneys, in the breaks between pain, there was something resembling happiness. Everybody will ask me about the deprivations, the 'terrors of the camps', but for me, the happiness there will always be the most memorable experience, perhaps. yes, that's what I'll tell them the next time they ask me: about the happiness in those camps.
If they ever do ask.
And if I don't forget.

Fateless
Imre Kertesz
trans. Christopher C. Wilson and Katharina M. Wilson
U.S.A. 1992, pp. 190-191

suit their own needs. The feeling created in the viewer - like the trauma the artists are dealing with - is personal.

The works in the exhibition are devoid of pathos or stereotype, because the formation of the image on the basis of memory does not reconstruct the story. Here meaning seeps through to the image from external knowledge to the work itself, giving impetus to the interpretation of hidden meaning. Reading the work is multi-faceted: are the *stripes* covering Moshe Kupferman's painting connected with his memories as a construction worker, his first occupation as a new immigrant arriving at a kibbutz, where he built wooden frames for houses and erected scaffolding? Or are they tenebrous witnesses to the railway tracks or barbed-wire fences?

Is the *red sand* in Micha Ullman's work an echo of the rich, red soil of his home town, Ramat Hasharon, or does it recall blood-drenched earth . . .

IF THIS IS A MAN

You who live safe In your warm houses,
You who find, returning in the evening
Hot food and friendly faces:
Consider if this is a man
Who works in the mud
Who does not know peace
Who fights for a scrap of bread
Who dies because of a yes or a no.
Consider if this is a woman,
Without hair and without name
With no more strength to remember,
Her eyes empty and her womb cold
Like a frog in winter.
Meditate that this came about:
I commend these words to you.
Carve them in your hearts
At home, in the street,
Going to bed, rising;
Repeat them to your children,
Or may your house fall apart,
May illness impede you,
May your children turn their faces from you.

If This Is a Man
Primo Levi
trans. Stuart Woolf
London, 1987, p. 17

Ariane Littman-Cohen's *beehives* look like a graveyard (in Hebrew, kever = grave, a masculine noun; kaveret = beehive, a feminine noun). Kever/kaveret are masculine/feminine; so is she saying something about the matriarchal world of the bees superseding the masculine memory of death?

Here we witness the blurring of borders between personal memory and collective historical memory. The latter passes through the filter of personal memory. In these art works, some of them serene and pleasing to the eye, it is difficult to differentiate between the memory of apocalyptic anxiety and the memory of quotidian anxiety; between the nightmare brought on by collective memory and the nightmare that is personal; between the memory of a generation that has perished, and the memory of a loved one that has died.

*This semiotic sequence has facilitated the acceptance of the memorial days by Israeli society, in spite of the near overlapping of Memorial Day with the eve of Independence Day which leaves no pause for the transition from mourning to rejoicing.
Israel Independence Day is celebrated on the day Israel was born, and is part of a series of commemorations: Holocaust Remembrance Day, Memorial Day for the fallen in Israel's struggle for survival; and Independence Day. These three days were arranged in linear order to construct a narrative continuum of Holocaust-Resistance-Rebirth parallel to historical fact: the near-destruction of the Jewish people, the struggle for survival and independence, and the attainment of statehood.

. . . it was in the midst of shouts rolling against the terrace wall in massive waves that waxed in volume and duration while cataracts of coloured fire fell thicker through the darkness, that Dr. Rieux resolved to compile this chronicle, so that he should not be one of those who hold their peace but should bear witness in favour of those plague-stricken people; so that some memorial of the injustice and outrage done them might endure; and to state quite simply what we learn in a time of pestilence: that there are more things to admire in men than to despise.

None the less, he knew that the tale he had to tell could not be one of a final victory. It could be only the record of what had had to be done, and what assuredly would have to be done again in the never-ending fight against terror and its relentless onslaughts, despite their personal afflictions, by all who, while unable to be saints but refusing to bow down to pestilences, strive their utmost to be healers.

And, indeed, as he listened to the cries of joy rising from the town, Rieux remembered that such joy is always imperiled. He knew what those jubilant crowds did not know but could have learned from books: that the plague bacillus never dies or disappears for good; that it can lie dormant for years and years in furniture and linen-chests; that it bides its time in bedrooms, cellars, trunks and bookshelves; and that perhaps the day would come when, for the bane and the enlightening of men, it roused up its rats again and sent them forth to die in a happy city.

The Plague
Albert Camus
trans. Stuart Gilbert
London 1948, pp. 284-285

The question of remembrance, however, remains important. We must remember not only the death chambers but also the rich complexity of Jewish life in Europe which died in them. Zionists resist reviving the memory of the life they rebelled against, but remembering the Holocaust requires a reevaluation of Zionist criticisms of the Jewish world that was destroyed. As for the form of remembrance, the only appropriate way to perpetuate the memory of the Holocaust is through meticulous documentation and mastery of facts. In the case of the Holocaust, The Devil is in the details.

"The uses of the Holocaust,"
Avishai Margalit
The New York Review of Books
February 17, 1994

Elisha Dagan

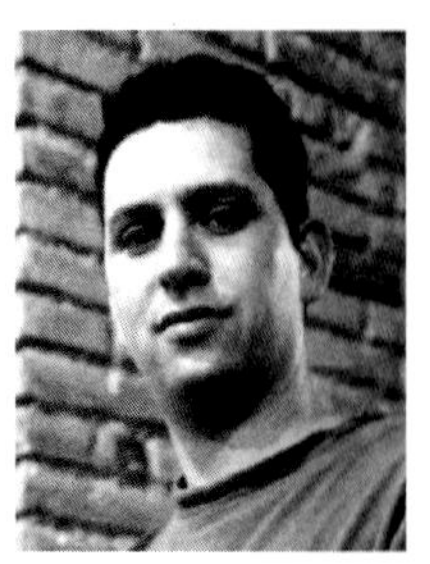

1961 *Born in Israel*
1984-1986 *Studied at the Bezalel Academy of Art and Design, Jerusalem*

SOLO EXHIBITIONS

1991 *"Western 2," Artifact Gallery, Tel-Aviv*
"West Side Stories," Arad Museum
1990 *"Reflection of Wind," the Bezalel Academy of Art and Design Gallery, Jerusalem*

GROUP EXHIBITIONS

1994 *"Halal - Contemporary Art From Israel," Sala 1, Rome*
1993 *"Eight Israeli Artists Recommended for the Aperto Venice 93," Artifact Gallery, Tel Aviv*
1992 *"Design Line Art," Museum of Israeli Art, Ramat Gan*
"Bezalel 88," Yavne Art Workshop Gallery, Yavne
1991 *"Contemporary Israeli Sculpture," Ilara Museum, Japan*
Artifact Gallery, Tel Aviv
"Israeli Art Now," Tel Aviv Museum of Art
"Young Artist Prize," Tel Aviv Museum of Art
"Imagewriting," Janco Dada Museum, Ein Hod
1990 *"Towards the 90's," Ein Harod Museum*
"The Next Generation," Artists Gallery, Tel Aviv

PRIZES

1992 *Jacques O'hana Prize for a Young Israeli Artist - Tel Aviv Museum of Art*
1991 *Young Israeli Artist Prize*
Beatrice S. Kolliner Prize for a Young Israeli Artist - Israel Museum
1988 *Ehud Elhanany Prize*

My works want to convey two things at once: real objects that exist here and now; and a dramatic adventure story told in headlines, a story in which time is a tangible factor in distinguishing between life and death, in leading from life to death.

If in my "stories" time is such a palpable, central factor leading from life to death that it must be made to stop moving, then my sculpture can be described as an attempt to plant a wedge that will stop the verbal-narrative process from reaching its end. Thus I assign a highly circumscribed role to the objects I create. It is not their task to tell stories, but rather to prevent stories from ending, by transmuting them into inanimate, frozen things. The task of these objects is to stop the wheel a moment before the end of the process of destruction, in spite of the knowledge that the destruction is inevitable.

1991

Western 4 (Go . . D), 1992

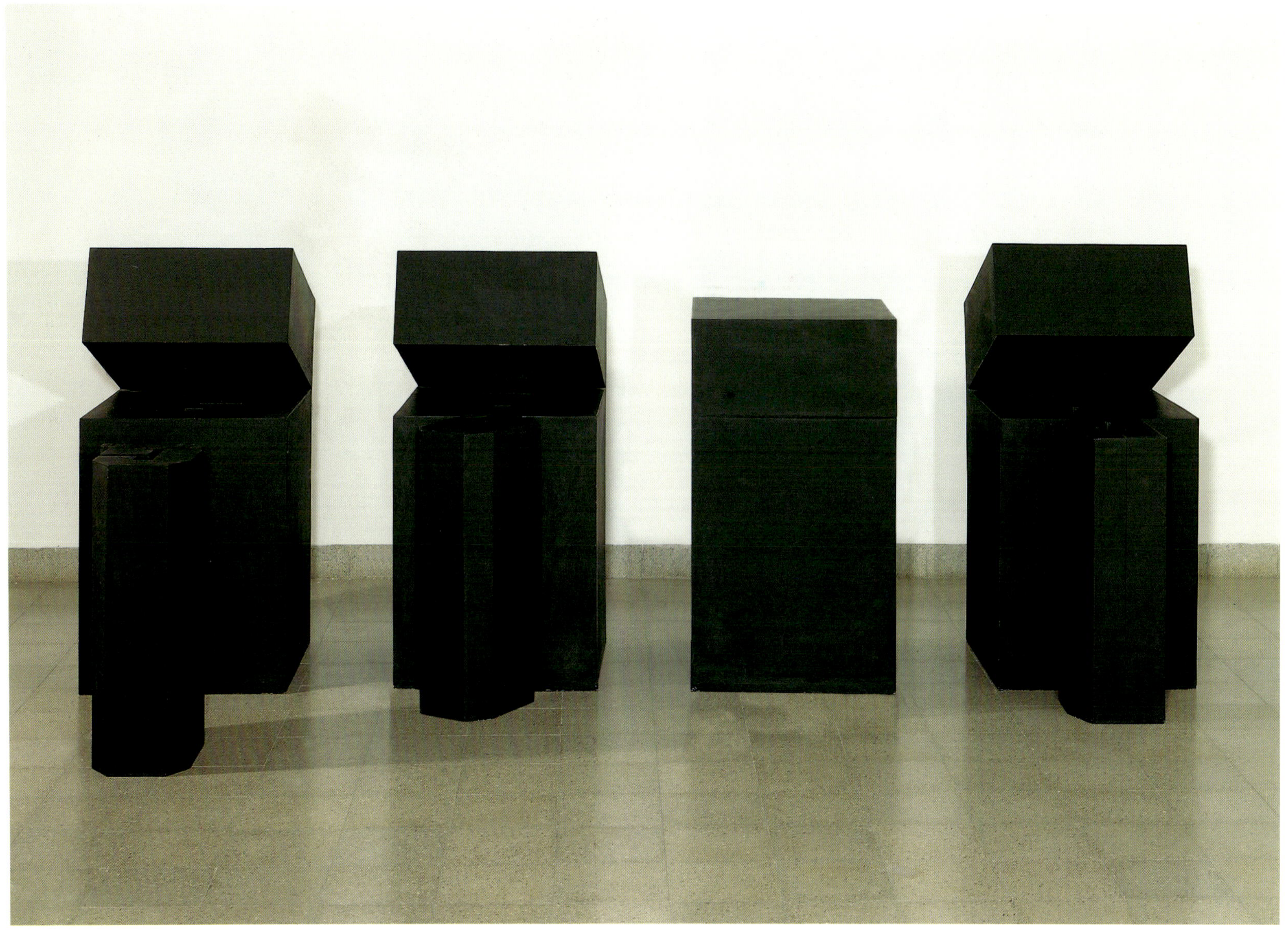

אלישע דגן

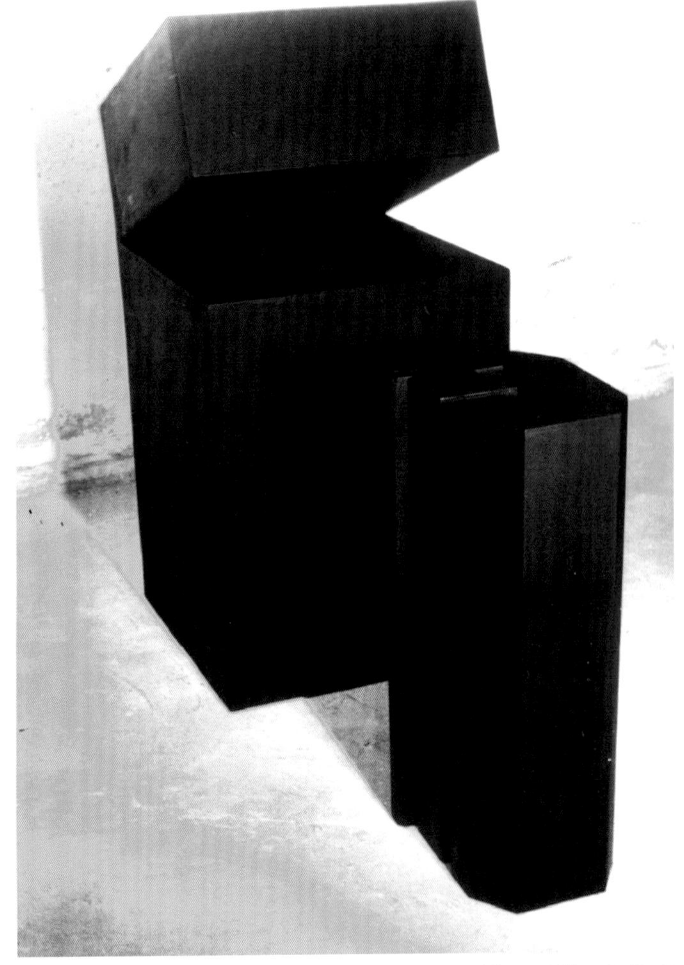

Westem 4 (Go . . D), (detail), 1992

העבודות שלי מתארות בעת ובעונה אחת שני מצבים: האחד – חפצים ממשיים, הנמצאים כאן, ברגע זה, והאחר – סיפור עלילה דרמטי, המתואר בראשי-פרקים, שהזמן מהווה בו מרכיב מהותי המבדיל בין חיים למוות, המוביל מן החיים אל המוות (1991).

כיוון שהזמן ב"סיפורים" שלי הוא מרכיב כה מהותי, הגורם העקרוני המוביל לחיים או למוות, הרי שעל הזמן הזה לעצור מלכת. אפשר, אם כן, לתאר את הפיסול שלי כניסיון לתקוע טריז, לעצור תהליך נאראטיבי-מילולי מלהגיע אל סופו. כך אני נותן, בעצם, תפקיד מוגדר מאד לאובייקטים שאני יוצר. תפקידם אינו לספר סיפור, אלא למנוע סיפורים מלהסתיים על-ידי הפיכתם לעצם דומם, קפוא. תפקידם של האובייקטים לעצור את הגלגל רגע לפני סופו של תהליך ההיתפָּלות, על אף הידיעה שאין ההיתפָּלות נמנעת (1991).

Ayana Friedman

Silent Environment

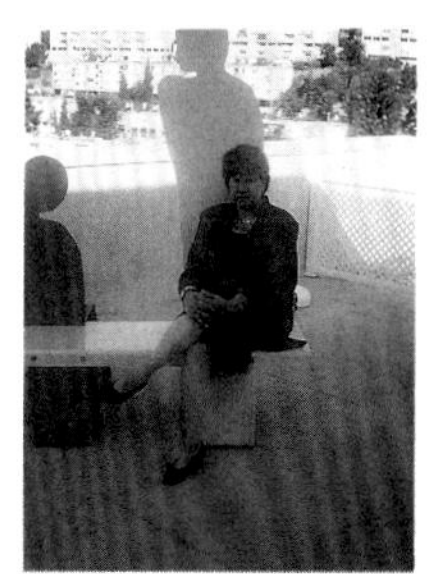

1950 *Born in Haifa, Israel*
1973 *B.A. History of Art and Hebrew Literature, Hebrew University of Jerusalem*
1980 *M.A. History of Art, Hebrew University of Jerusalem*
1982-84 *Studies at John F. Kennedy University, Fiberworks Center for the Textile Arts, Berkeley*
1988-89 *Graphic Art Studies at City College, San Francisco*

TEACHING EXPERIENCE

1995 *Guest lecturer, Beersheba Teachers Seminary, "The Role of Curator in Israeli Art"*
1994- *Lecturer, Ministry of Foreign Affairs, course for diplomat corps cadets*
1977-1996 *Teacher, Israel Museum, adult education*
1974 *Teaching Assistant, Hebrew University of Jerusalem, Department of Art History*

SPECIAL EVENTS

1994- *Curator, Navon Gallery, Neve Ilan*
1993 *Assistant Curator of the exhibition, "Homage to Julia Keiner-Forchheimer," Israel Museum, Design and Architecture Department*
1989-93 *Published articles in the journals Studio and Mishkafayim. Reviewer of art and art exhibitions for the newspapers Al-Hamishmar and Kol Yerushalayim*
1982-83 *Guest curator in the Design and Architecture Department, Israel Museum, Jerusalem*
1978 *First Prize in Sculpture, awarded by the History of Art Department and the Institute for the Humanities, Hebrew University of Jerusalem*
1974 *Participant in the workshop of Dr. Zion Avital, "Artonomy, Systemic Art," Hebrew University, Jerusalem.*

SOLO EXHIBITIONS

1993 *Artists House, Jerusalem*
1991 *Tova Osman Art Gallery, Tel Aviv*
1990 *Sculpture exhibition at Hyperkol Talpiot, Jerusalem*
1986 *Dugit Gallery, Tel Aviv (Fiber Art)*
1983 *Fiberworks Gallery, Berkeley*
1981 *Hakibbutz Gallery, Tel Aviv (Fiber Art)*

GROUP EXHIBITIONS

1994 *"And the Ship Sails On...," Navon Gallery, Neve Ilan, an ArtFocus Exhibition*
"Passages," Navon Gallery, Neve Ilan
1992 *Six Rooms Gallery, Tel Aviv*
1989 *Fort Mason, San Francisco, (Drawing)*
1982 *"Touch," Israel Museum (Soft Sculpture)*
1981 *Center for Visual Arts, Beersheba*
"Political Identity," Hakibbutz Gallery, Tel Aviv
1974 *O'hana Gallery, London (Outdoor Sculpture)*
1971-73 *Students Group Exhibitions, Wise Bldg. and National Library Bldg., Hebrew University of Jerusalem*

In this installation, there are four photos of performance artist Adina Bar-On, posed and photographed by Ayana Friedman.

During the process of creation, the artist was directed to push her face and body up against a large pane of glass, creating the impression of crushing, pressure and blows.

The photos were enlarged and printed on soft cloth, and then sewn together with a blanket and stuffed with synthetic cotton to create a comforter, a warm and embracing protective covering.

The blankets hanging on the wall bring to mind "womanly" arts such as quilting. The room, padded with scenes of a stifled scream, evokes a room in a mental ward, whose padded walls are meant to protect the patient from him/herself.

The image of the woman is trapped between a hard glass wall and a soft cloth, and yet she strives to escape, to extricate herself. Her cry is visible but silent, expressing acute distress, suffering.

The cry and struggle to escape are symbolic. It is the cry of the lost childhood of my mother, a Holocaust survivor, persecuted for many years, tormented by her memories even now. The stifled cry evokes her nightmarish experience, and is also the stifled fear of the children of Holocaust survivors, a fear from which they yearn to be delivered.

At the entrance to the room, on the wall, on a small sign: The viewer is invited to walk through this installation touching, feeling, experiencing the physical material. The sculpture environment is transformed into theater in which the viewers are the actors, and the sculpture, the scenery.

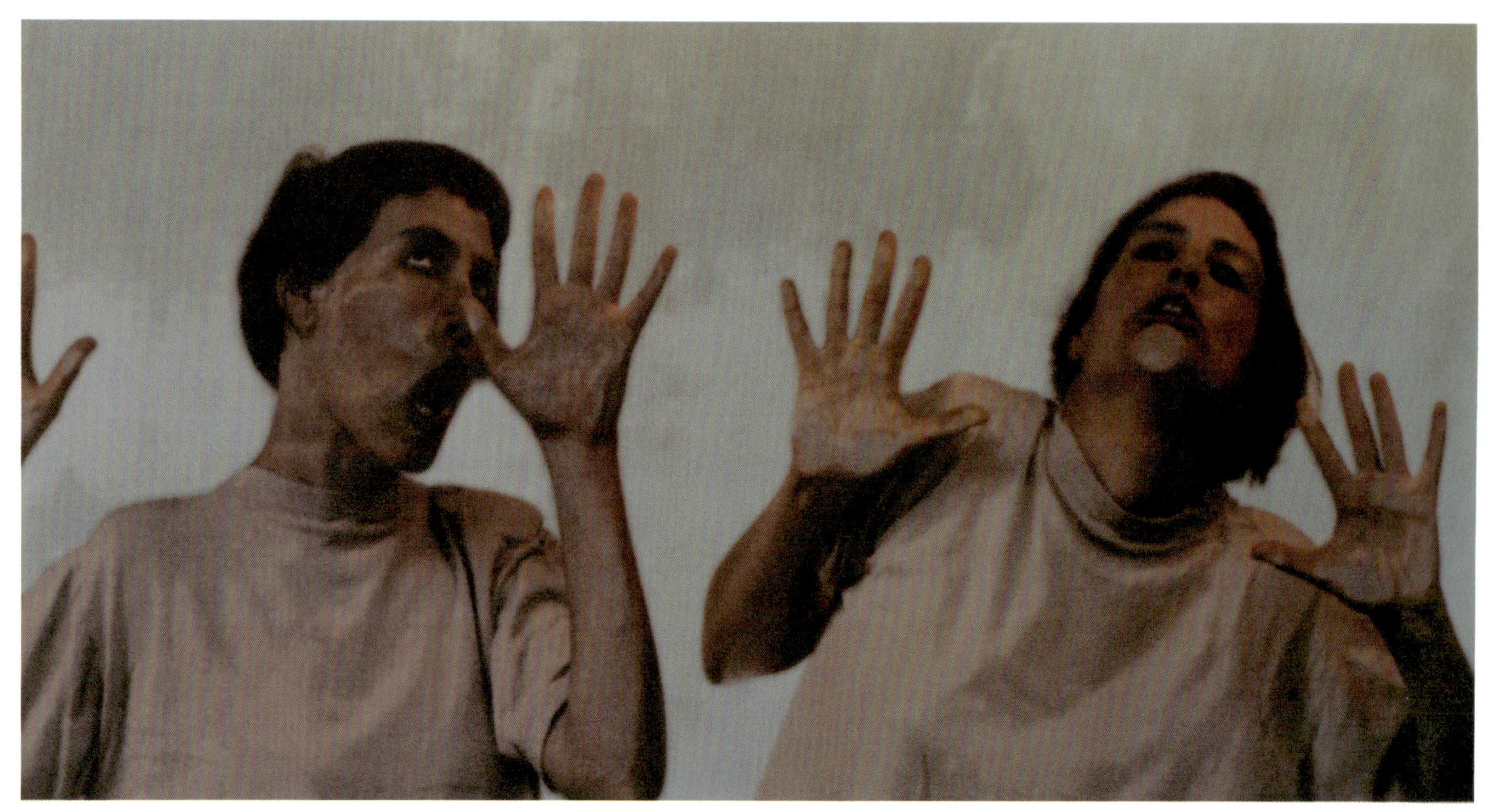

Silent Environment, (detail),
1996
סביבה שקטה, (פרט)

עיינה פרידמן

סביבה שקטה

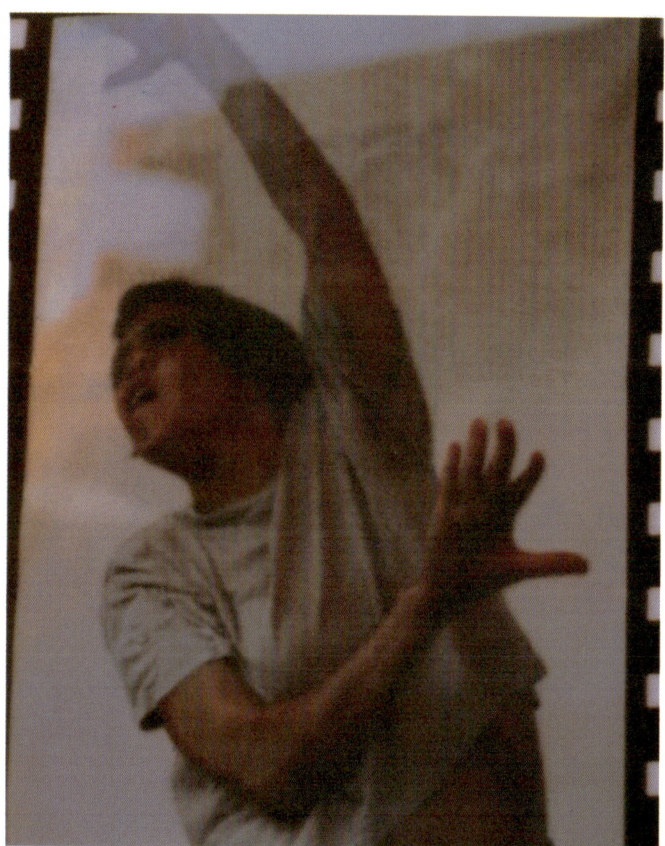
Silent Environment, (detail), 1996
סביבה שקטה, (פרט)

במיצב זה ארבעה תצלומי ענק של אשה. הדמות המצולמת היא אמנית המיצב עדינה בר-און.

בתהליך העבודה לחצה האמנית את עצמה כנגד קיר זכוכית גדול, ובכך יצרה באברי גופה ובפניה סימנים של מעיכה, מכה ולחץ.

התצלומים הודפסו על בד רך ונתפרו לאחר ההדפסה לשמיכה רכה ממולאת בצמר גפן סינטטי, כמין שמיכת פוך. השמיכה מתקשרת בתודעת הצופה לעטיפה מגוננת, מחממת ומחבקת.

השמיכות התלויות על הקיר מתקשרות גם לאומנויות ״נשיות״, למשל קווילטינג. החדר המרופד במראות של זעקה חנוקה מעורר אסוציאציה של חדר בבית חולים לחולי רוח, שקירותיו המרופדים אמורים להגן על החולה מפני עצמו.

דמות האשה כלואה בין דופן הזכוכית הקשה לבין הבד הרך, ועם זאת, היא מנסה לצאת ולמלט את עצמה מן המלכודת. הזעקה אילמת, רק היא נראית לעין, והיא מבטאת עינוי ומצוקה חריפה.

הזעקה והמאבק להיחלצות סימליים. הזעקה היא זעקת הילדות האבודה של אמי, ניצולת השואה, שנרדפה שנים רבות וגם עתה היא עדיין נרדפת על ידי זכרונות העבר. הזעקה החנוקה היא זכר ללילות של חלומות הביעותים, הזעקה היא גם זעקת הפחד החנוק, שאתו גדלים ילדי הדור השני לשואה, ושממנו הם שואפים להיחלץ.

Moshe Gershuni

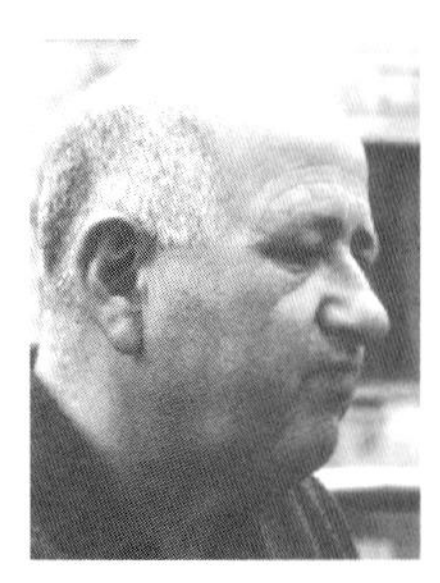

1936 *Born in Tel Aviv*
1960-64 *Studied at Avni Art Institute, Tel Aviv*
1972-77 *Teacher at Bezalel Academy of Art and Design, Jerusalem*
1978 *Teacher at Art Teachers' Training College, Ramat Hasharon*

SELECTED SOLO EXHIBITIONS (since 1985)

1996 *Galerie Hubertus Wunschik, Düsseldorf*
Galerie Hubertus Wunschik, Monchengladbach
"The Next of Kin," Schwabish Gemund
1995 *Bezalel Academy of Art and Design, Jerusalem*
"The Next of Kin," European Cultural Center, Thuringen, Erfurt (with Shlomo Koren)
1994 *Givon Gallery, Tel Aviv*
Galerie Hubertus Wunschik, Düsseldorf
1993 *Galerie Michael Hadinclever, Munich*
Galerie W. Asperger, Strasbourg
Artists' Studio Gallery, Tel Aviv
Museum of Israeli Art, Ramat-Gan
1992 *"I know," Givon Gallery, Tel Aviv*
1990 *Overbeck-Gesellschaft, Lubeck, Germany*
Deson-Saunder Gallery, Chicago
Works 1987-1990, Tel Aviv Museum of Art
1989 *Gimel Gallery, Jerusalem ("The Green Series")*
Deson-Saunder Gallery, Chicago
Michael Hasenclever Gallery, Munich
1988 *Thirteen Etchings for Poems by C.N. Bialik, Tel Aviv Museum of Art*
"Jewish Ceramics," Bezalel Academy of Art, Jerusalem
1987 *"Painting on Paper," Michael Hasenclever Gallery, Munich*
"Budapest Series," Art Workshop Gallery, Jerusalem
Givon Gallery, Tel Aviv
"For My Brethren and Companions' Sakes," Bezalel Academy of Art, Jerusalem
1986 *"For man and beast are creatures of chance", Israel Museum, Jerusalem*
1985 *"Etchings and Silkscreens," Noemi Giron Gallery, Tel Aviv*
Kibbutz Lohamei Hagetaot
Kibbutz Cabri
Mishkenot Sha'ananim, J. Robert Fisher Hall, Jerusalem

SELECTED GROUP EXHIBITIONS (since 1986)

1995 *"Look Who's Talking - View of Israel Art," Hubertus Wunschik Gallery, Düsseldorf*
"Deutschsein?" Stadtische Kunsthalle Düsseldorf
"From Inside Out," Jewish Museum, New York

"There are no more Jews," announced the old woman . . .The sun was full and low, and a silence, like after a great war, was spread on the valley . . . Everything has stopped moving . . . " (Aharon Appelfeld, **Katarina**, Norton & Co., New York, 1993, p. 186).

There is a similarity between the feeling evoked by Appelfeld's lines and the one evoked by looking at Moshe Gershuni's works. The full and low sun, the silence after war has ended, the universe that has stopped moving: as though the splendor of the last sunrays in Appelfeld's words and in Gershuni's works allude to what came before the silence, before the end.

These paintings seem eventless. Most of the canvas surface is covered with brilliant yellow shades that partly conceal an underlying lumpy, coarse layer of pale gray. Parts of this layer are visible as thick, visceral chunks; others disappear, almost completely absorbed by the bright yellow surface. The thick, saturated chunks are the sources of paint drips pulled downward and upward with equal energy. This vertical movement intersects with horizontal paint bands, stopped only, it would seem, by the work's invisible frame.

The yellow intensity gives a sense of suffocation, as though the color were sealing a world that was there once but is no longer penetrable. Against this thick materiality, which seems to strain at covering up a ruined world, the vigorous paint drips resemble a torrential rain that changes the surface of the earth, causing the sewers to overflow and sweeping along the entire culture of Europe. But from where Gershuni stands, the beneficial European rain changes into "a yellow wind, a hot and terrible east wind, a wind that will come from the gate of Hell . . . After that day . . . the land will be covered with bodies. The rocks will be white from the heat, and the mountains will crumble into a powder which will cover the land like yellow cotton . . ." (David Grossman, **The Yellow Wind**, Picador, London, 1988, pp. 75-76).

Gershuni's sealing and obliteration could also be interpreted as an act of mapping - mapping a place that has just been covered. On the one hand the "place" is there yet invisible and defying representation; on the other hand it is here, without limits or rules, as an expression of memory only. The Gershuni who conceals the facts from himself - and from us - reveals his emotions in the coexistence of light and horror, making us

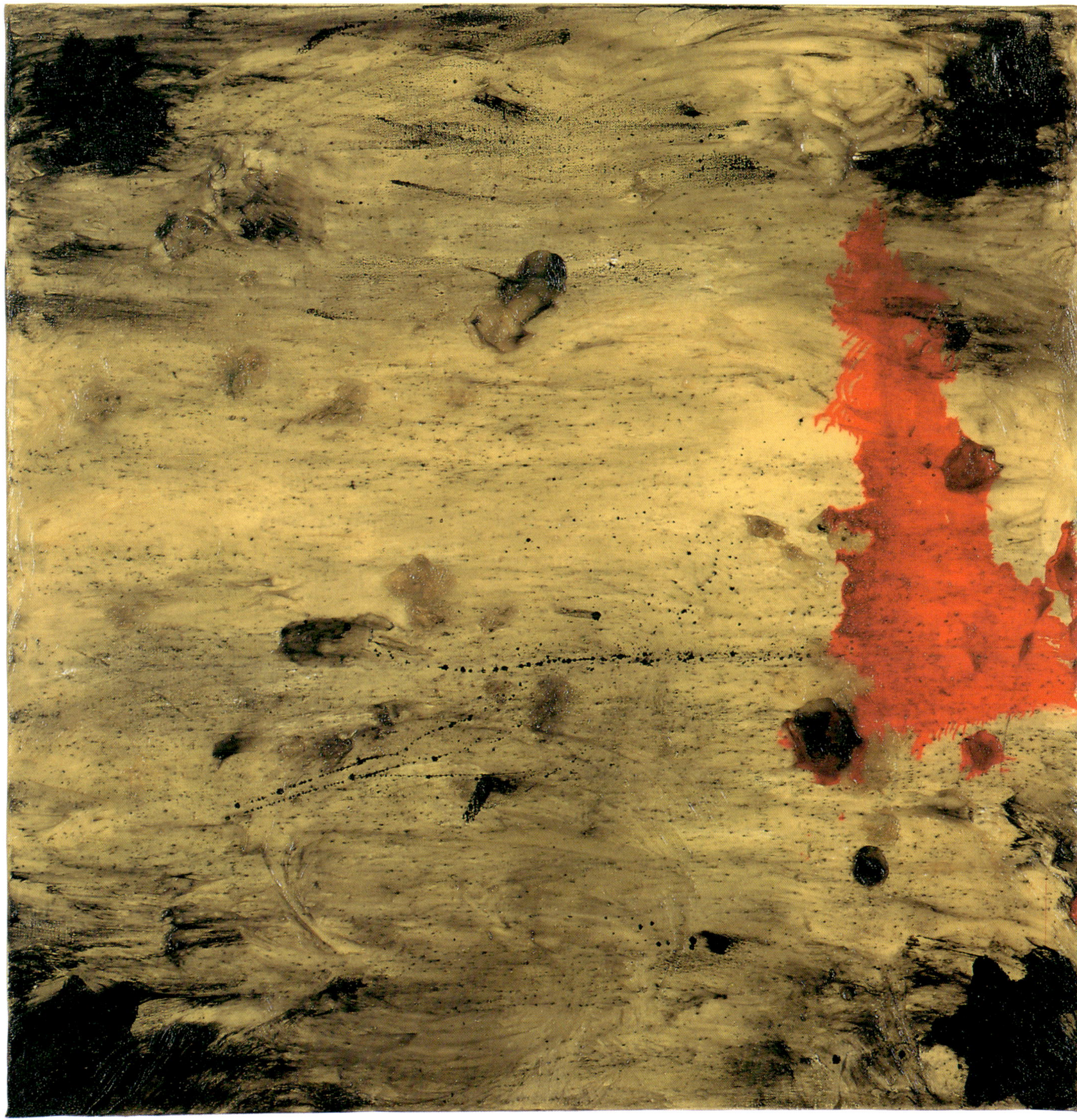

Untitled, 1994
ללא כותרת

1994	*"Building Bridges," Meridian Center, Washington*
	"The Printers Imprint" Israel Museum, Jerusalem
	"Along New Lines: Israel Drawing Today," Israel Museum, Jerusalem
	"Anxiety," Museum of Israeli Art, Ramat Gan
	"Grosse Kunstausstellung NRW," Kunstpalast, Düsseldorf
1993	*"Look Who's Talking - View of Israel Art," Galerie Hubertus Wunschik, ehem "Delta Galerie" Düsseldorf*
	"Deutschsein ?" Stadtische Kunsthalle Düsseldorf
	"From Inside Out," Jewish Museum, New York
1992	*"Positions Israel" Collection Dr. R. Hocherl/W. Asperger, Kunstlerbaus Bethanien, Berlin*
	"Routes of Wandering," Israel Museum. Jerusalem
	"Combined Painting - collage object," Noemi Givon Gallery, Tel Aviv
1991	*"Art in Israel Today," Detroit Institute of Arts, Michigan*
1990	*"Print Today," Artist's House Tel Aviv*
	"Drawing and Beyond," Givon Gallery, Tel Aviv
	"Drawing Material," Gimel Gallery, Jerusalem
	"The Jewish Experience in the Art of the Twentieth Century," Barbican Art Gallery, London
	"On Paper/In Paper/With Paper," Israel Museum, Jerusalem
	Israel Art Around 1990 - Israel U.S.S.R.
1989	*"Israeli Art," Svea Gallery, Stockholm*
	Jarl Borgens Collection, Silkborg Art Museum, Denmark
	"In the Shadow of Conflict," Jewish Museum, New York
	"Les Magiciens de la terre," Centre George Pompidou, Paris
	"Etchings for Poems," Jerusalem Print Workshop. Jerusalem
	"Jerusalem Print Workshop, A Decade of Printmaking," Tucson Museum of Art, Arizona
1988	*C. Majorkas Collection, Copenhagen*
	Haifa Portrait of the City, Haifa Museum of Modern Art
	"Judaica - Here and Now," Israel Museum, Jerusalem
	"The Binding of Isaac in Israeli Art," Museum of Israeli Art, Ramat Gan
	"Black/White, Ben Ari Museum, Bat Yam
	"A People Builds Its Land," Herzliya Museum
	"Man Has Many Images," Museum of Israeli Art, Ramat Gan
	C. Majorkas Collection Zug, Switzerland
	"Israeli Art," Foreign Office Shows, Sweden, Finland
	"Artist/Format," Museum of Israeli Art," Ramat Gan
1986	*"The Want of Matter - a Quality in Israeli Art," Tel Aviv Museum of Art*
	"Israeli Art," Centro Cultural de la Villa Madrid
	Palao Robert, Barcelona

PRIZES

1989	*Kolb Prize, Tel Aviv Museum of Art*
1988	*Minister of Education and Culture Prize for Painting and Sculpture*
1982	*Sandberg Prize, Israel Museum, Jerusalem*
1969	*Aika Brown Prize, Israel Museum, Jerusalem*

sway between attraction to the light's intensity and repulsion by the horror's intensity.

In a work from 1988 Gershuni used a verse from the prayer intoned during the Jewish funeral procession: "Justice shall walk before him." The work features four white porcelain plates, chipped and cracked, arranged with strict precision. Each plate is emblazoned with a swastika surmounted by the German eagle. The artist paints a thick black swastika on the top two plates while inscribing "Justice shall walk before him" across the bottom two. The adjacent yellow spot refers to the yellow Star of David.

Since the Hebrew word inscribed in this work is not vowelled, it could be read as either "Sham" (There) or "Shem" (Name). In one work Gershuni includes two names alluding to "there/name," yet lacking an explicit signifier. Another possible reading is that the word "Hashem," meaning God, has been "beheaded," that is, it appears without the definite article "ha" (the). In this sense the format of the cross created by the unfolded shoe box pits the Christian sign against the absence of God: "Thou shalt not take the name of the Lord thy God in vain: for the Lord will not hold him guiltless that taketh his name in vain" (**Deuteronomy** 5:11).

In his use of "Sham" and "Shem" Gershuni pits the private against the public. The upper center features three cigarette butts that form a triangle surrounding, as on a tombstone or in a heraldic sign, a small mound of ashes. Are we to see these as human remains of Holocaust victims? And below - cinders, remains of the ashes of others. The Shem/Sham inscription appears in the center, with red poured on most of the surface from the center outward.

A sense of private and public comes across. On the one hand, separation from a dear one by his grave and a last farewell to "There" (Sham). On the other hand, separation from "There" or burial of the "Shem," while we stay on. The "There" whose heraldic sign is on the tombstone, like a keystone holding up a house, remains in our historical memory as a place where a part of our people and heritage have been buried.

Nella Cassouto

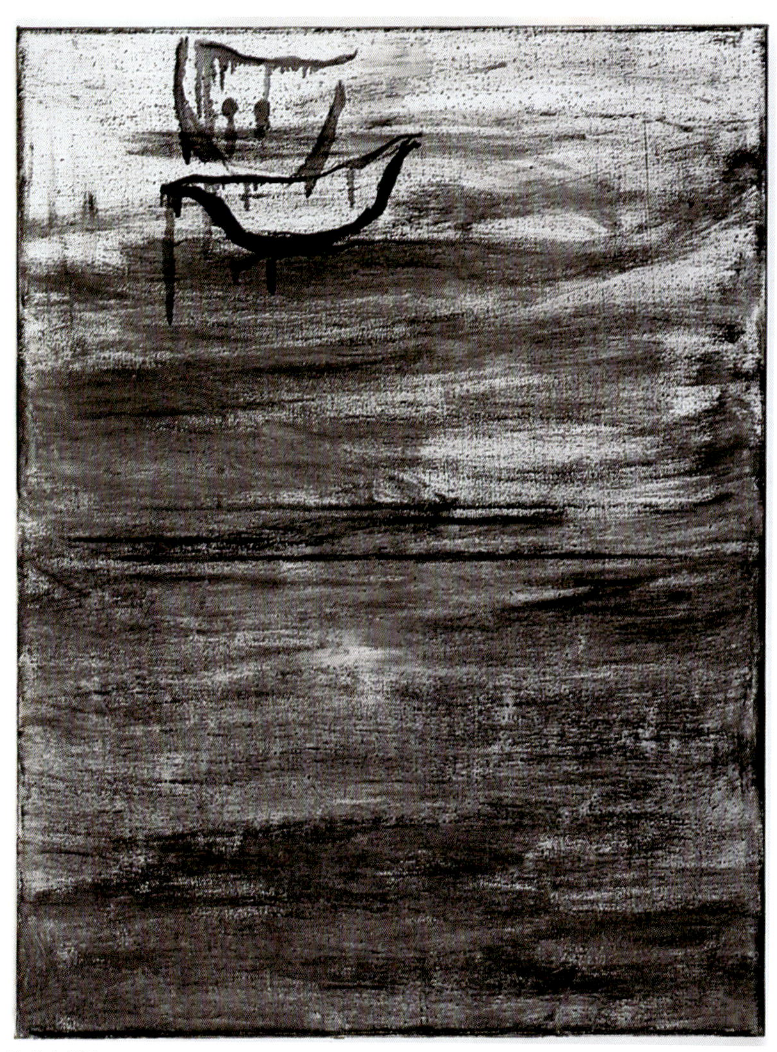

Untitled, 1994
ללא כותרת

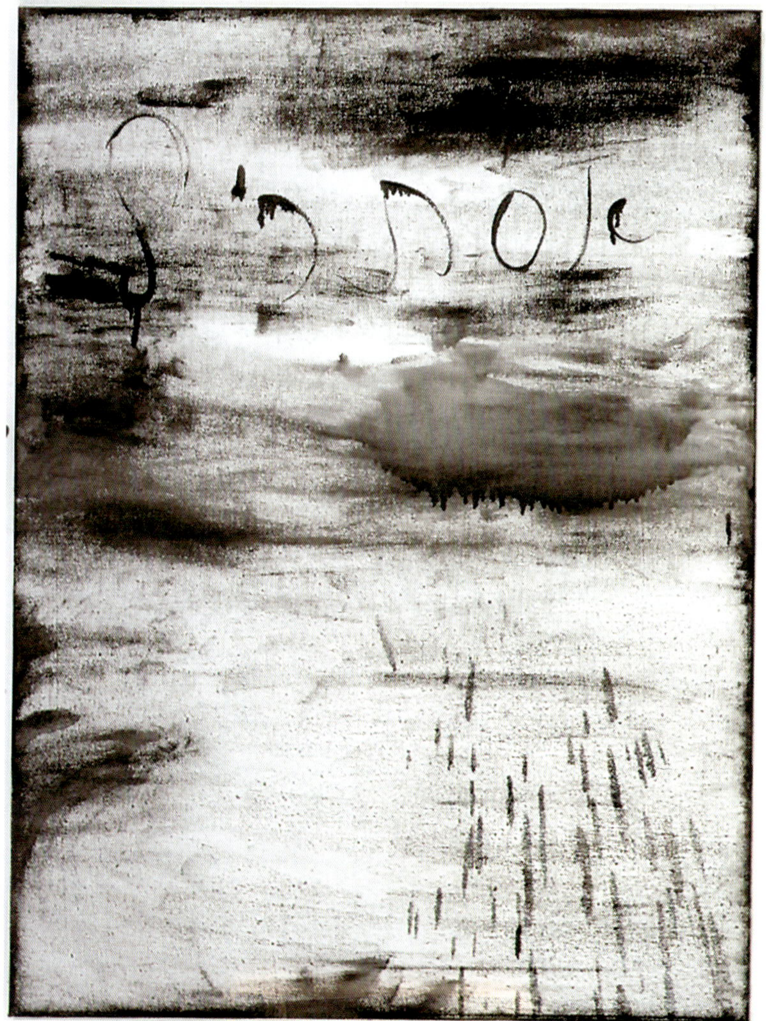

Esther I, 1994
אסתר'ל

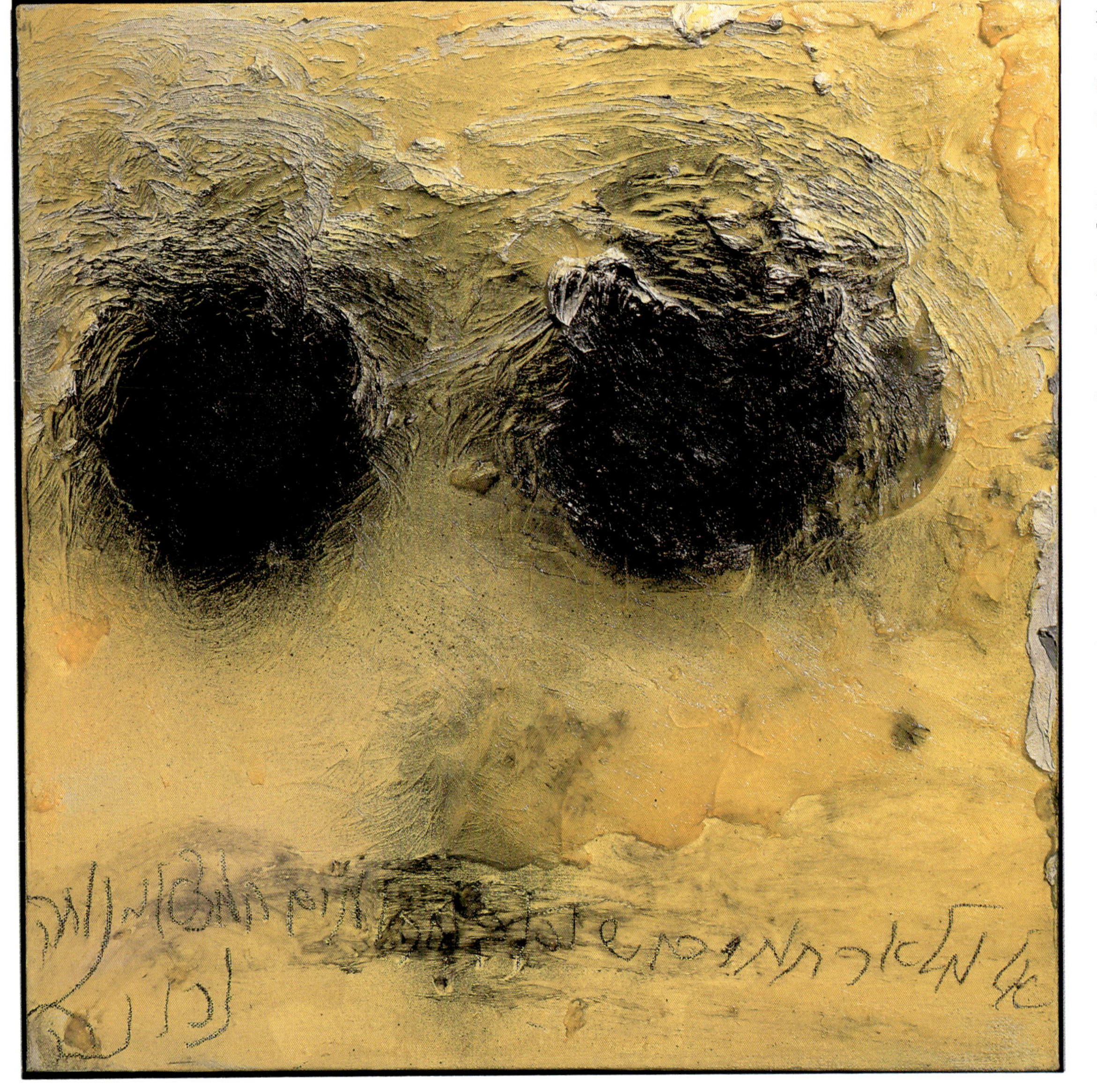

"שֵם". בעבודה אחרת כולל גרשוני שני שמות הרומזים ל"שָם/שֵם", אך חסר מסומל מפורש. עוד אפשרות לקריאת מילה זו היא המילה ה-שם, כלומר אלוהים, ש"נערפה", שהופיעה כביכול ללא ה' הידיעה.

אם נפרש זאת כך, הרי שהצלב שנוצר מקופסת הנעליים הפתוחה מעמיד את הסמל הנוצרי אל מול היעדר אלוהים, כפי שכתוב בספר דברים (פרק ה', 11): "לא תישא את שם יהוה אלהיך לשוא כי לא ינקה יהוה את אשר ישא את שמו לשוא" ועוד: "כי אם אל המקום אשר יבחר יהוה אלהיכם מכל שבטיכם לשום את שמו שם לשכנו תדרשו ובאת שמה" (**דברים** יב', 5).

בשימוש שעושה גרשוני ב"שָם" ו"שֵם" הוא מעמיד את הפרטי אל מול הציבורי. במרכז החלק העליון של התמונה שלושה בדלי סגריות היוצרים משולש מסביב לערימת אפר קטנה. האם עלינו לראות בו את שרידי קרבנות השואה? ומתחת – אודים, שאריות מאפרם של אחרים. הכתובת שם מופיעה במרכז, באדום השפוך על מרבית השטח מן המרכז כלפי חוץ.

תחושת הפרטי והציבורי מתערבבות זו בזו. מצד אחד, פרידה ממישהו יקר ליד קברו וברכת שלום אחרונה ל"שם". ומצד שני, פרידה מן ה"שם" או קבורת ה"שם", בעוד אנו ממשיכים לחיות. ה"שם" ששלטו הנישא נמצא על המצבה, כאבן פינה בבית, נותר בזכרון ההיסטורי שלנו כמקום שבו חלק מעמנו וממורשתנו נשאר קבור.

נלה קסוטו

משה גרשוני

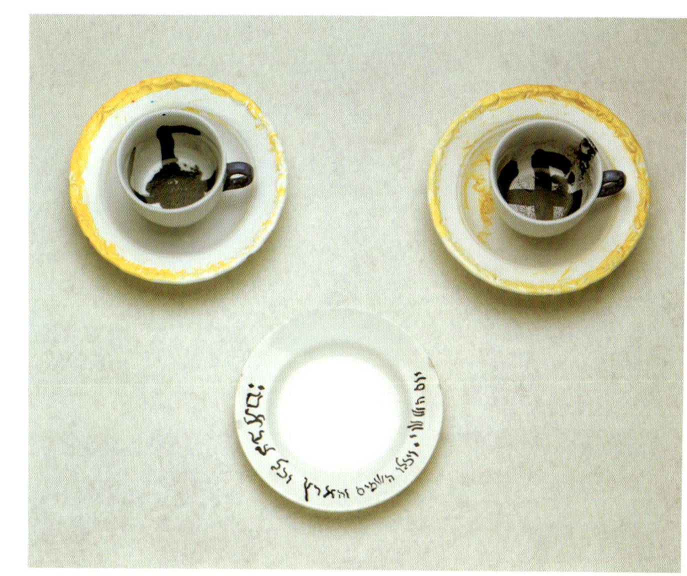

The Sixth Day, 1988
יום השישי

God Full of Mercy, 1996
אל מלא רחמים

"אין עוד יהודים, הודיעה האשה הזקנה...השמש היתה עגולה ונמוכה, ודממה, כמו אחרי מלחמה גדולה, היתה פרושה על העמק...הכל עצר מלכת..." (אהרון אפלפלד, **קאטרינה**, ניו-יורק 1993, עמ' 119).

יש דמיון בין התחושה המתעוררת למקרא שורותיו של אפלפלד לבין זו המתעוררת למראה עבודותיו של משה גרשוני. השמש העגולה והנמוכה, השקט שלאחר המלחמה, היקום שאינו זע; כאילו זוהר קרני השמש האחרונות במילותיו של אפלפלד ובעבודותיו של גרשוני רומזות רמז למה שהיה פעם, לפני הסוף.

דומה שהציורים חסרי אירועים. רוב שטחו של הבד מכוסה בצללים צהובים מבהיקים המכסים באופן חלקי שכבה גושית ומחוספסת של אפור חיוור. חלקים משכבה זו נראים כפרוסות קרביים עבות, אחרים נעלמים, נבלעים כמעט לגמרי ומתמוססים בכיסוי הצהוב הבוהק. הפרוסות העבות הרוויות הן מקורות טפטופי צבע הנמשכים מעלה ומטה בכוח שווה. תנועה אנכית זו נחתכת על-ידי פסי צבע אפקיים, הנעצרים כאילו במסגרת הבלתי נראית של התמונה.

האינטנסיביות הצהובה גורמת להרגשת מחנק, כאילו היה הצבע חותם לעולם שהיה שם לפנים אך אין לחדור אליו עוד. אל מול החמריות הבוטה הזו, שדומה שהיא מנסה בכל כוחה להסתיר עולם חרב, נראים טפטופי הצבע האנרגטיים כמבול המשנה את פני האדמה, הגורם לתעלות הביוב לעלות על גדותיהן ולהציף את תרבות אירופה כולה. אך מן המקום שבו עומד גרשוני, גשם הברכה האירופי הופך ל"רוח צהובה...משער הגיהנום... והיא רוח מזרחית חמה ואיומה,...אחרי יום שכזה,...תהיה הארץ מכוסה גוויות. הסלעים יהיו מלובנים מרוב החום, וההרים יתפוררו לאבקה שתרבץ על הארץ ככותנה צהובה." (דויד גרוסמן, **הזמן הצהוב**, 1987, עמ' 46).

אך החתימה וההכחדה של גרשוני יכולות להתפרש גם כפעולה של מיפוי – מיפויו של מקום שאך זה כוסה. מצד אחד, ה"מקום" הוא שם, מקום בלתי נראה עדיין הדורש שיציגוהו; ומצד שני, המקום הוא כאן, ללא גבולות או חוקים, כביטוי הזכרון בלבד. הצייר גרשוני המסתיר את העובדות מעצמו – ומאתנו – מגלה את רגשותיו בקיומם יחד של האור והאימה, והוא גורם לנו להתנודד בין משיכת האור החזק לבין האימה הגדולה.

בעבודה משנת 1988 השתמש גרשוני בפסוק הנאמר בזמן טקס ההלוויה היהודי, "צדק ילך לפניו". בתמונה מוצגות ארבע צלחות חרסינה לבנות, פגומות וסדוקות, מסודרות בקפידה. על כל צלחת חרות צלב-קרס ומעליו סמל הנשר הגרמני. האמן מצייר צלב-קרס שחור ועבה על שתי הצלחות העליונות וכותב "צדק ילך לפניו" על פני שתי הצלחות התחתונות. הנקודה הצהובה הנספחת היא תזכורת לטלאי הצהוב.

כיוון שהמלה העברית הכתובה ביצירה זו אינה מנוקדת, אפשר לקראה או "שָׁם", או

Moshe Kupferman

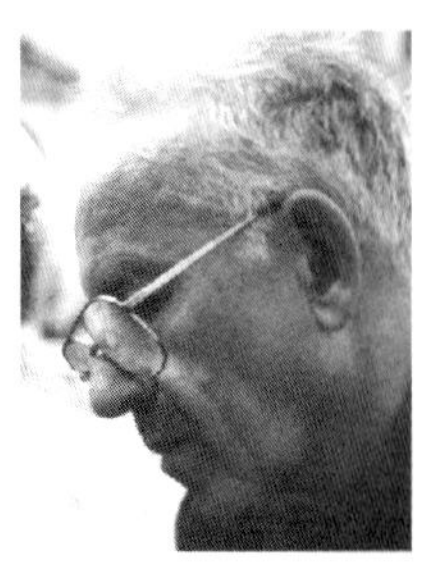

1926 Born in Jaroslav, Poland
lives on Kibbutz Locahmei Hagetaot, Israel

SELECTED SOLO EXHIBITIONS

1996 New Works at Lohamei Hagetaot Gallery
1994 Studio Bocchi, Rome
1993 Muzeum Sztuki, Lodz and Centrum Sztuki Wspolczesnej, Warsaw
Works on Paper, Malarstwo/Painting
1992 Noemi Givon Gallery, Tel Aviv
Shigeru Yokota Gallery, Tokyo
1991 "Between Oblivion and Remembrance: Paintings and Works on Paper, 1972-1991," North Carolina Museum of Art, Raleigh
Musée d'Art Contemporain, Dunkirk
1987 "Peintures et oeuvres sur papier," Musée national d'art moderne, Centre Georges Pompidou, Paris
1984 "Paintings, Works on Paper, 1963-1984," Israel Museum, Jerusalem, and Tel Aviv Museum of Art
1981 "Works on Paper," Stedelijk Museum, Amsterdam
1980 "Matrix 61," Wadsworth Atheneum, Hartford, Connecticut
1978 Tel Aviv Museum of Art
1977 "Five Paintings, Nine Drawings," Bertha Urdang Gallery, New York
1969 Israel Museum, Jerusalem
1962 Ghetto Fighters' House, Kibbutz Lohamei Hagetaot
1960 Chemerinsky Gallery, Tel Aviv

SELECTED GROUP EXHIBITIONS

1995 Carnegie International, Carnegie Museum, Pittsburgh
"Where is Abel Thy Brother ?" Galeria Zacheta, Warsaw
1994 "Along New Lines: Israeli Drawing Today," Israel Museum, Jerusalem
1993 "Jacob Elhanani and Moshe Kupferman: Drawings," Centre des Arts Saidye Bronfman, Montreal
1991 "Routes of Wandering: Nomadism, Voyages and Transitions in Contemporary Israeli Art," Israel Museum, Jerusalem
"Art in Israel Today," Detroit Institute of Arts
1989 "Transformations in Landscape: Postwar Works from the Collection," Albright-Knox Art Gallery, Buffalo, New York
"In the Shadow of Conflict: Israeli Art, 1980-1989," Jewish Museum, New York
1986 Venice, XLII Esposizione Internazionale d'Arte: La Biennale di Venezia
"The Want of Matter: A Quality in Israeli Art," Tel Aviv Museum of Art
1985 "Kunst in Israel 1960-1985," Koninklijk Museum voor Schone Kunsten, Antwerp
1984 "Drawings, 1974-1984," Hirshhorn Museum and Sculpture Garden, Smithsonian Institution, Washington, D.C.
1981 "Artists of Israel: 1920-1980," Jewish Museum, New York
1978 "Seven Artists in Israel: 1948 -1978," Los Angeles County Museum of Art

"First I put in emotion and expression.
Then I cover them up.
Then I put in silence."

For the viewer who stands facing a work by Moshe Kupferman, there exists the possibility of executing a kind of reversal of the process performed by the artist - to remove the veil of silence, to peel away the various layers and coverings, thus restoring the emotion and the expression present at the beginning. Kupferman's work must be seen as a process in time, layer upon layer, image upon image, and a development of states.

Kupferman says: "It is possible for a painter, in his work, to traverse - each time, with each canvas separately - the entire way. The existence of each additional work will be justified when one more step has been added to this 'entire way'. The existence of time, what happens inside it and what happens to us through it, must be present in everything."

Kupferman's painting is about preserving the memory of this entire process. He adds: "We are the captives of our times - but also their partners and contributors. That's how it is in good times or bad, for good or ill. For me, the canvas is a field, the field where everything accumulates, everything happens, everything of weight and value is found, as I am capable of absorbing and expressing it. The picture is that same "everything" that is summed up in a moment of concentration, of effort, and of grace.

From the painter - expert and committed witness - wonder is not concealed. But at the same time, the memory of all that is terrible and frightful in our time is equally rooted in my memory.

A painter may travel the whole road in each and every one of his works. The existence of each additional work will be justified by its adding yet another step to the "whole road" traversed. This is essential because the curiosity to receive the picture in its next condition overwhelms the tendency to preserve what has already been achieved and acknowledged. I am an artist who does not choose the subject of his work. I have no subjects. There is only time, what happens in it, and what happens to us in it.

The result is a multi-layered painting that recalls and expresses times, memories, situations, and values simultaneously. In such a painting the finished picture is, in the last analysis, an interrupted situation -

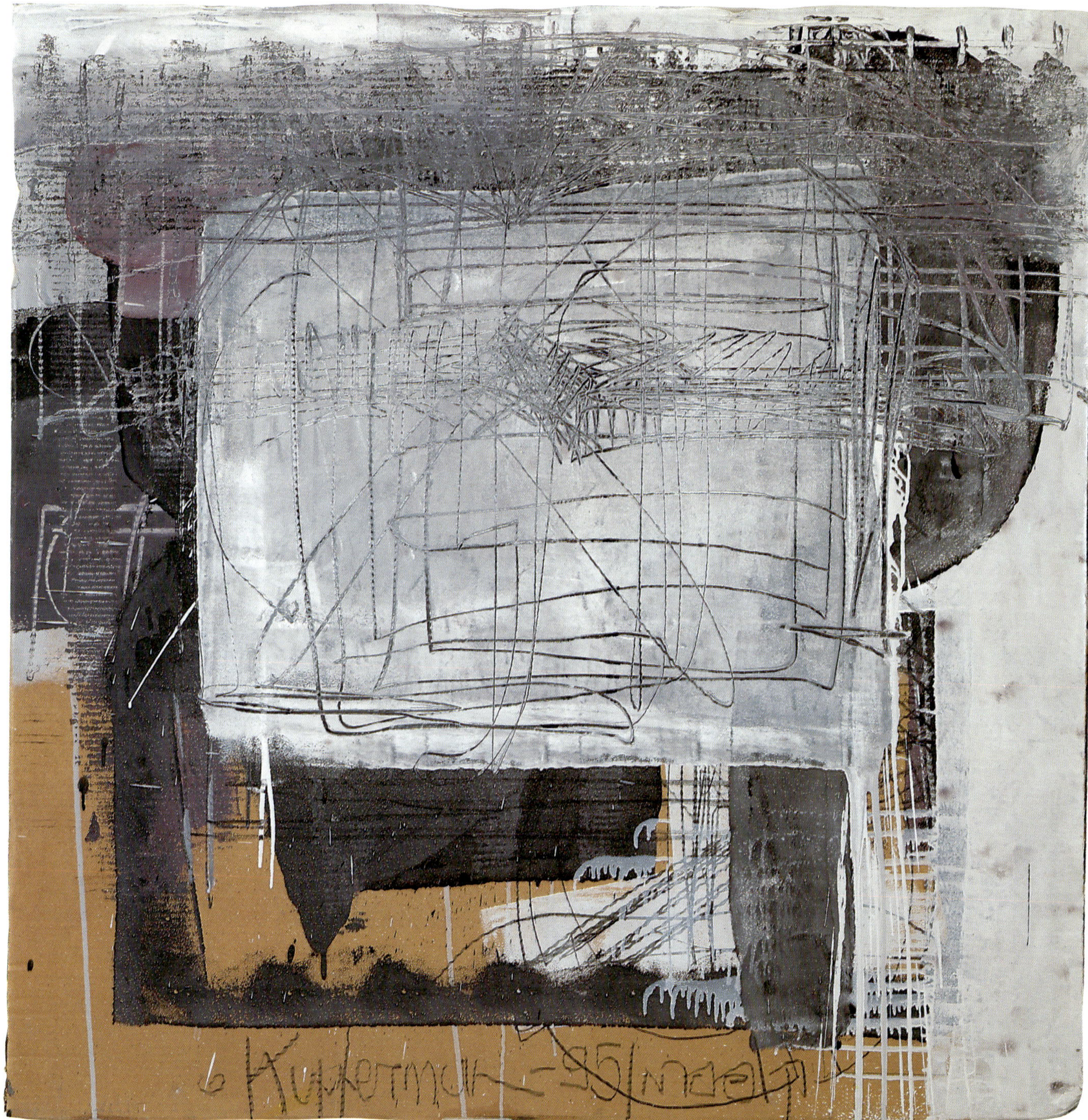

Industrial Cardboard, 1995
קרטונים

1977 *"10 kunstere fra Israel," Louisiana Museum of Modern Art, Humlebaek, Denmark*
1975 *"Three Israeli Artists: Gross, Neustein, Kupferman," Worcester Art Museum, Massachusetts*
1974 *"Beyond Drawing," Israel Museum, Jerusalem*
1963 *"New Horizons," Mishkan Leomanut, Museum of Art, Ein Harod, Israel*

approved (by its creator), and it somehow presents us with the all-at-one-time. This multifaced painting that results from the process paint-erase-paint-add, a process of build-destroy-build created while developing and consolidating a personal technique must in the end give us both the personal and the periodic."

Nella Cassouto

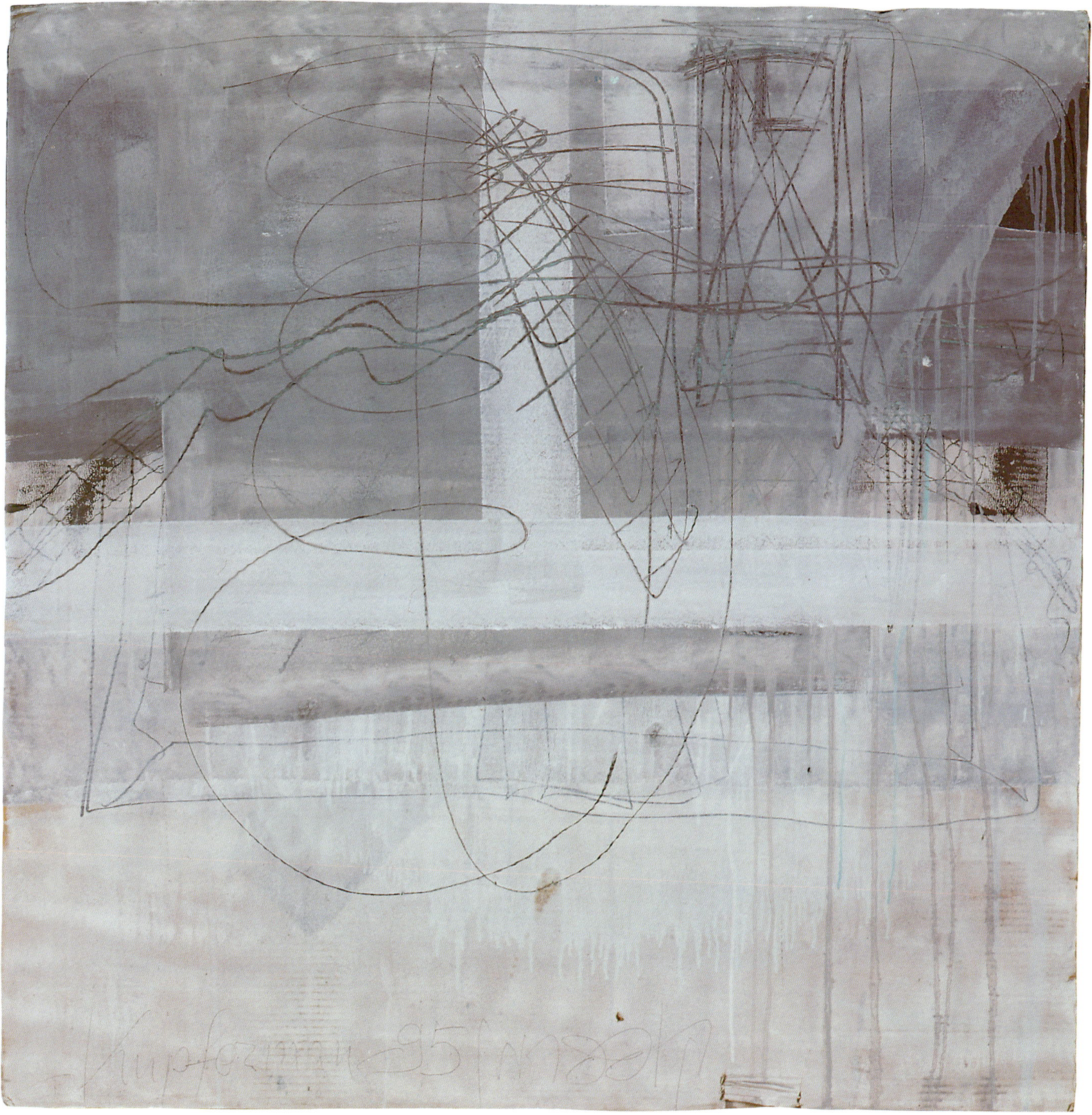

Industrial Cardboard, 1995
קרטונים

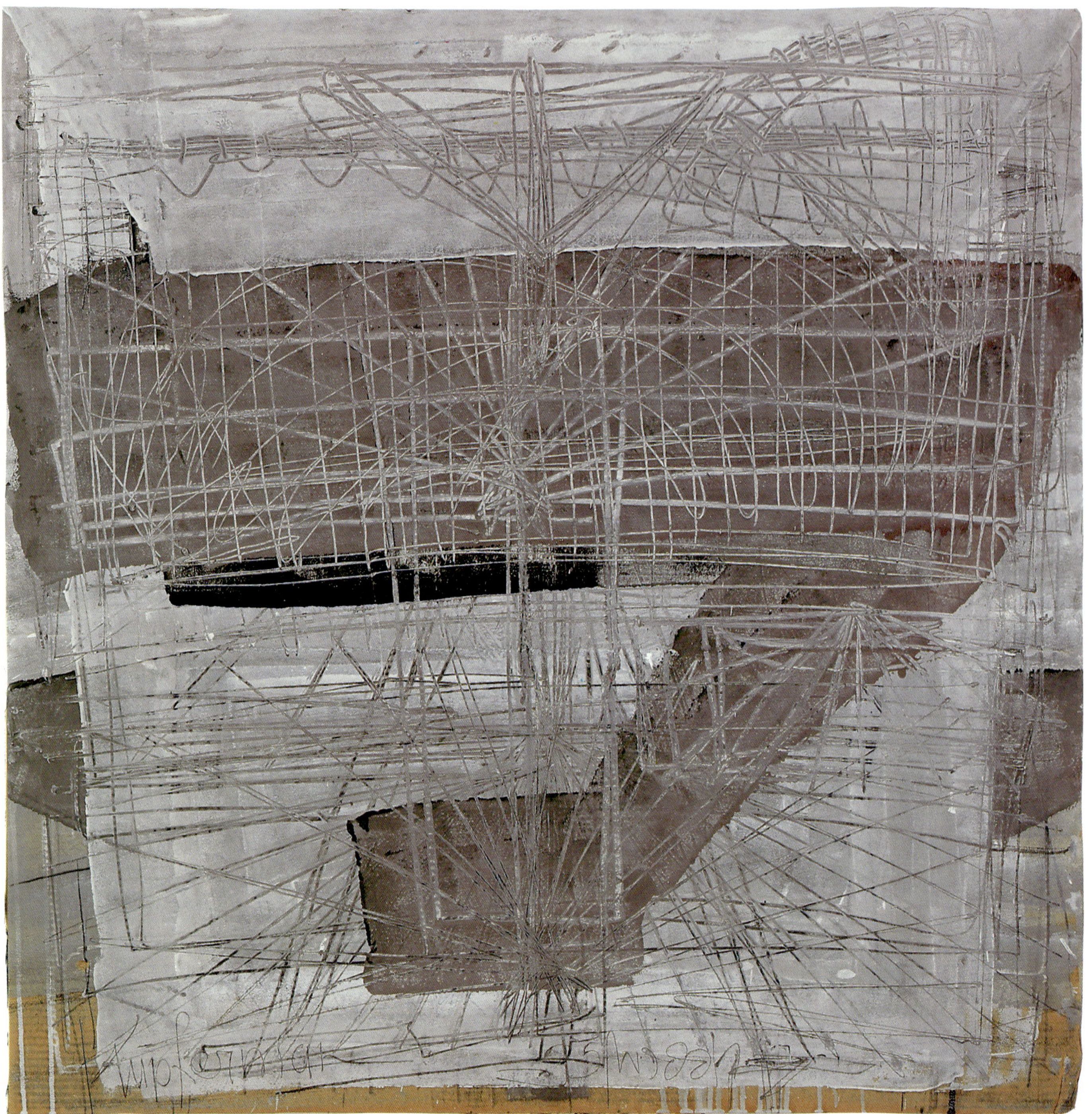

Industrial Cardboard, 1995
קרטונים

משה קופפרמן

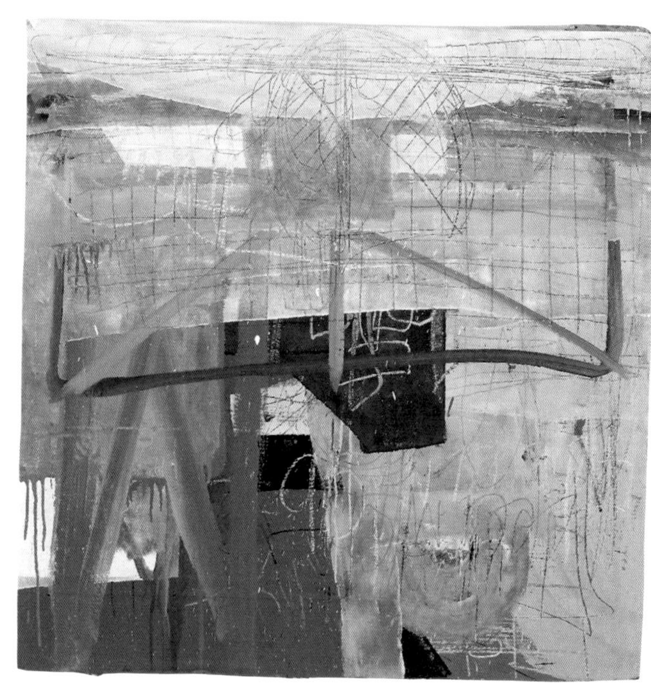

Industrial Cardboard, 1995
קרטונים

"תחילה אני נותן ביטוי לרגשות.
אחר-כך אני מכסה אותם.
ואז, אני מוסיף את השתיקה."

הצופה העומד לפני תמונה של משה קופפרמן, יכול לבצע פעולות אלה, אך בסדר הפוך – תחילה להסיר את מסך השתיקה, אחר כך לקלף את הכיסויים והשכבות השונות, וכך להחזיר שנית את הרגשות ואת הביטוי המצוי בתחילת בריאתה של התמונה.

יש לראות את יצירתו של קופפרמן כתהליך המתרחש בזמן. שכבה על גבי שכבה, תמונה על גבי תמונה והתפתחות של מצבים. כך מבטא זאת הצייר:

"...הננו שבויי זמננו, אבל גם שותפים-תורמים שלו. כך זה בטוב וברע, לטוב ולרע. בשבילי בד הציור שדה הוא, שדה כל המצטבר, כל המתרחש, כל בעל המשקל והערך, כפי שאני מסוגל לקלוט ולהעלות. התמונה הינה אותו "הכל", כפי שהוא מסתכם ברגע של ריכוז, של מאמץ ושל חסד.

צייר, עד-זוכר ומחוייב, לא נסתר ממני המופלא; אבל, ולא פחות מכך, רובץ עלי זכרון כל הנורא והמעורר אימה של תקופתנו.

...אפשר שצייר יעבור בעבודתו, בכל פעם, על כל בד בנפרד ובכל תמונה בודדת, את הדרך כולה. קיומה של כל עבודה נוספת יוצדק בכך שעל "הדרך כולה" נוספה עוד פסיעה...

הכרחי הוא שהסקרנות לקבל את התמונה במצב הבא שלה תגבר על הנטיה לשמור את שהושג כבר ונמצא ראוי. הנני צייר העושה במלאכה ואינו בוחר את נושאיו. אין לי נושאים. קיים הזמן, מה שקורה בו ומה שקורה לנו בו... מה שמתקבל בסופו של דבר הוא ציור רב-שכבתי המעלה ומביע זמנים, זכרונות, וגם ערכים – כל אלה מיוצגים בו-בזמן. בציור כזה התמונה הגמורה היא, בסיכומו של דבר, מצב מופסק-מאושר (על ידי יוצרה), והיא מטפלת ומגישה לנו באופן כלשהו את הכל-לאותו-זמן. הציור רב הפנים הזה המתקבל בתהליך של מעלה-מוחק-מעלה ומוסיף, תהליך שהוא גם בונה-הורס-בונה, הנוצר תוך פיתוח וביסוס של טכניקה אישית-פרטית, חייב לתת בסופו של דבר גם את האישי וגם את התקופתי."

ציוריו של קופפרמן הם אודות שמירת זכרון תהליך זה בשלמותו.

נלה קסוטו

Ariane Littman-Cohen

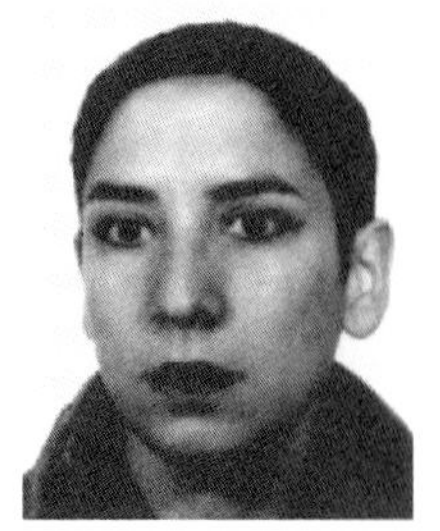

1962 *Born in Switzerland*
1981 *Immigrated to Israel, lives in Jerusalem*
1982-1986 *BA, International Relations and the History of Muslim Countries, Hebrew University of Jerusalem*
1987-1991 *Studied at and graduated with honors from the Bezalel Academy of Art and Design, Jerusalem*
1991-1994 *Assistant Curator of Contemporary Art, Israel Museum, Jerusalem*
1996 *Postgraduate Studies, Bezalel Academy of Art and Design, Jerusalem, and Art Department, Hebrew University of Jerusalem*

SELECTED SOLO EXHIBITIONS

1996 *Series of Contemporary Art Exhibitions, Herzliya Museum of Art*
1995 *"Virgin of Israel and her Daughters," Artists House, Jerusalem*
1992 *"Nature Morte," Bograshov Gallery, Tel Aviv*

SELECTED GROUP EXHIBITIONS

1996 *"Desert Cliche: Israel in the 90's Local Images," The Bass Museum, Miami Beach*
"Marks - Artists WorkingThroughout Jerusalem," Israel Museum, Jerusalem
1995 *"New Works," Noga Art Gallery, Tel Aviv*
"Sculpture, Installation 95" Israel Festival, Jerusalem
1994 *"Meta-Sex 94," Bat Yam Museum*
"Bograshov the Street - Export Surplus," Bograshov Gallery, Tel Aviv
"Tel Hai -94," Upper Galilee
"90. 70. 90," Tel Aviv Museum of Art, Helena Rubinstien Pavilion for Contemporary Art
"Meta-Sex 94," Mishkan Leomanut, Ein Harod
"From the Collection," Israel Museum, Jerusalem
"Bograshov 3, The Suitcase," Bograshov Gallery, Tel Aviv
1993 *"The Range of Realism," Tel Aviv Museum of Art*
Sharett Foundation Grant Winners, The Genia Schreiber University Art Gallery, Tel Aviv
"Third Person," Bograshov Gallery, Tel Aviv
1992 *"Who is signed on the duck?" Bograshov Gallery, Tel Aviv*
1991 *Bezalel, Academy of Art and Design, Jerusalem*

PRIZES

1992 *America - Israel Cultural Foundation Grant for Young Artist*
1991 *Bezalel Academy Marie Fisher Memorial Prize for the Advancement of Young Artists*

The encounter with beehives is usually unexpected. One might come upon them while walking in open fields, far from populated areas, while the busy traveler might, at best, catch a glimpse of them from his speeding car or train. Except for the devoted beekeeper, few of us will ever approach those simple boxes, buzzing with life, which both attract and arouse a feeling of awe.

Symbol of the "terrible," this matriarchal monarchy with more than 30,000 members has a thirty-million-year-old complex social history as well as an association with man dating back to prehistoric times.

Exhibited here, in their dim red light, opened and emptied of their combs, stripped down of all "danger," the hives still bring forth associations of vessels of death. Such associations, formalistic at first sight, have roots in our collective memory, at a time when the ancients invested the bee with chthonian characteristics connecting it with the birth and death of the soul, while honey was connected everywhere with the ritual of the dead. On the other hand, the bee also represented the more positive side of the feminine archetype, as the embodiment of the feminine potency of nature, symbolizing the motherliness of earth, with its never-resting quality and expressing its motherhood in the nursing bees which fed the infant Zeus with honey, the purest product of organic nature.

Here in the gallery the viewer can take a safe stroll around those open wombs, allowing his eye to slowly wander inside the hive, discovering the mysterious traces of a presence now gone.

Each hive, symbol of man's love for order and above all of man's domestication of nature, offers us a personal testimony of this ghostly presence which reflects the dialectic of the nature-culture relationship. Signs of the quality of randomness contrast sharply and sometimes even violently with the minimalistic orderly quality of the hive.

Those beautiful and disturbing "designs" are the imprints left by the deadly presence of the Golem, still to grow and develop into a dangerous enemy: the wax-moth. This parasite, using the combs' construction to create a weblike tunnel as a protection from danger, will feed on combs, honey, and eggs, eventually signaling the death of the entire colony.

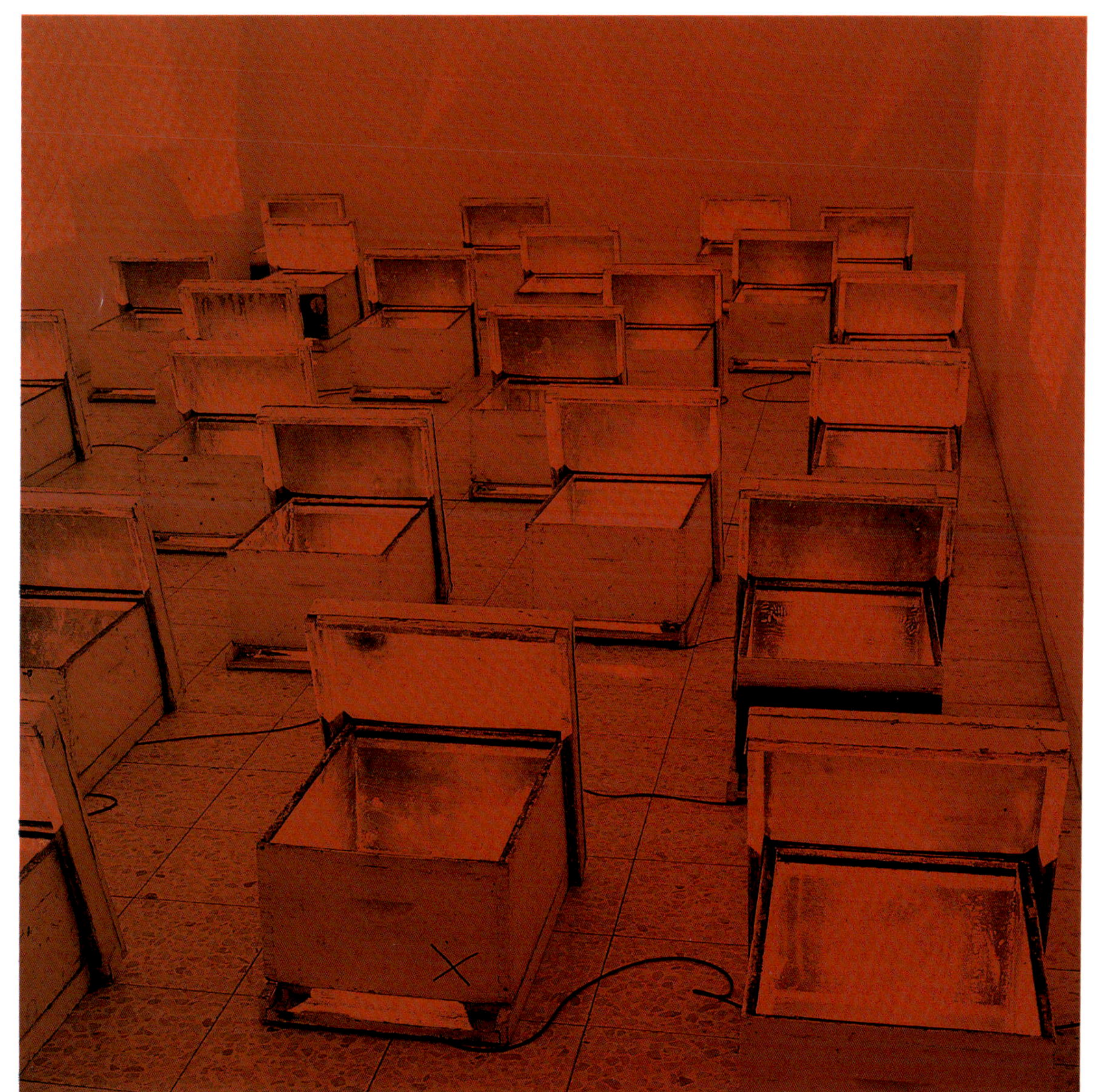

It is now, in their still and grave purposelessness, that those empty hives allow for a possible aesthetic feeling to arise in the viewer, an aesthetic of death whose origin is Nature itself which has left its stamp on this cultured object, an object both offered to and reflecting our gaze.

March 1996

Virgin of Israel and Her Daughters, 1994
בתולת ישראל ובנותיה

אריאן ליטמן-כהן

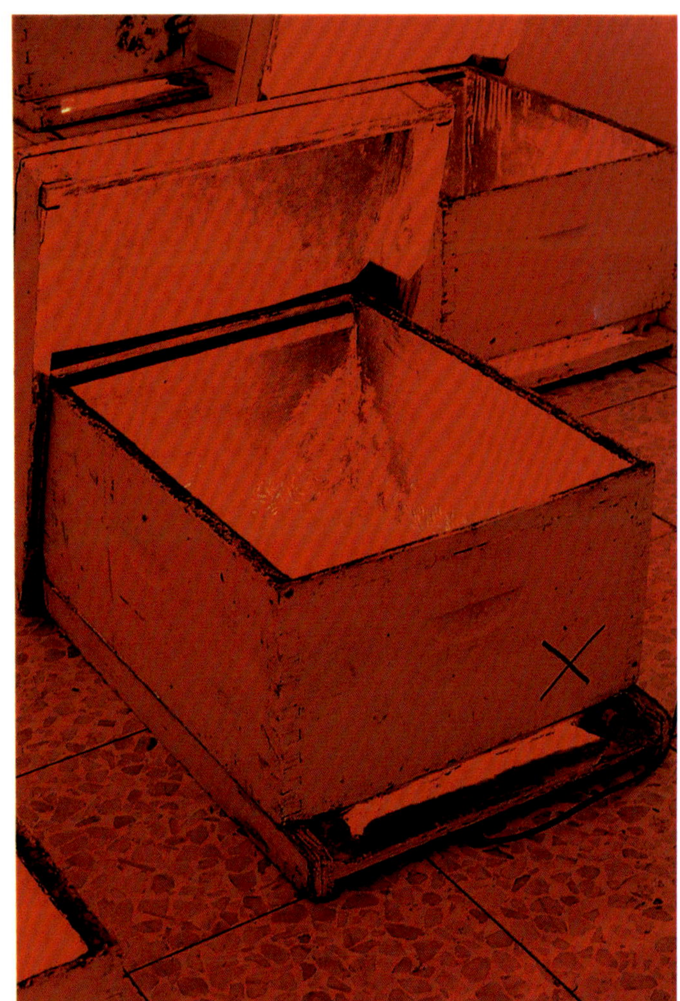

Virgin of Israel and Her Daughters, (detail) 1994
בתולת ישראל ובנותיה (פרט)

בדרך-כלל ההיתקלות בכוורות דבורים איננה צפויה. יש הנתקל בהן בטיילו בשדה הפתוח, הרחק ממקום יישוב; הנוסע הטרוד יקלוט, לכל היותר, בזווית עינו משהו מהן בעברו במהירות במכוניתו, או בישבו ברכבת הדוהרת. לבד מן הכוורן המסור, מעטים יתקרבו לארגזים הפשוטים הללו, ההומים חיים, המושכים ומעוררים חרדה בעת ובעונה אחת.

סמל ה"נורא", לממלכה המטריארכלית הזו המונה יותר מ-30,000 פרטים בתוכה, היסטוריה חברתית מורכבת של יותר משלושים מיליון שנה ויחסים הדדיים עם האדם שתחילתם בזמנים פרהיסטוריים.

הכוורות המוצגות כאן באורן האדמדם העמום, פתוחות ומרוקנות מחלות הדבש, מפורקות מכל "סכנה", עדיין מעוררות בדמיון מחשבה על כלי-קיבול שמוות בתוכם. הקשרים כאלה, הנראים פורמליסטיים במבט ראשון, שרשים להם בזכרון הקולקטיבי שלנו, מזמן שהקדמונים ייחסו לדבורה תכונות שטניות וקישרוה ללידת הנשמה ולמותה, והשתמשו בדבש בפלחן המתים. מצד שני, הדבורה אף ייצגה את הצד החיובי של האב-טיפוס הנשי, את התגלמות הפוטנציאל הנשי של הטבע; היא סימלה את אימהותה של האדמה שאינה נחה לעולם וביטויה בדבורים שהזינו את זאוס בדבש – המוצר האורגני הטהור ביותר שבטבע.

כאן בגלריה יכול המתבונן לטייל בביטחה סביב כוורות-הרחם הפתוחות, להרשות לעיניו לסקור לאיטן את פנים הכוורת, ולגלות את הסימנים המסתוריים של נוכחות שאיננה עוד.

כל כוורת, המסמלת את אהבת האדם לסדר ומעל לכל את יכולתו לביית את הטבע, הינה עדות אישית לנוכחות-צללים זו המשקפת את הדיאלקטיקה של יחסי הטבע-התרבות. סימנים בעלי אופי של שרירותיות עומדים בניגוד חריף ולעתים אף אלים לאופי המינימליסטי המסודר של הכוורת.

ה"ציורים" היפים והמטרידים הללו הם טביעות שהשאירה נוכחותו הממיתה של הגולם, טביעות שיש בכוחן לגדול ולהתפתח שוב לאויב מסוכן: עש-השעווה. טפיל זה, העושה שימוש במבנה חלות הדבש, יוצר רשת מחילות המגינה עליו מפני סכנה, בעודו ניזון מן החלות, הדבש והביצים – ובכך הוא גוזר מוות על מושבת הדבורים כולה.

רק עתה, במצבן הדומם וחסר התועלת, יכולות הכוורות הריקות לעורר בלב המסתכל את ההרגשה האסתטית, את תחושת האסתטיקה של מוות שמקורו בטבע עצמו; הטבע הוא שהשאיר חותמו על החפץ המתורבת הזה, חפץ המוצע לעינינו ובה-בעת מחזיר לנו מבטנו כבבואה.

מרס 1996

Meeting Daniel Sack

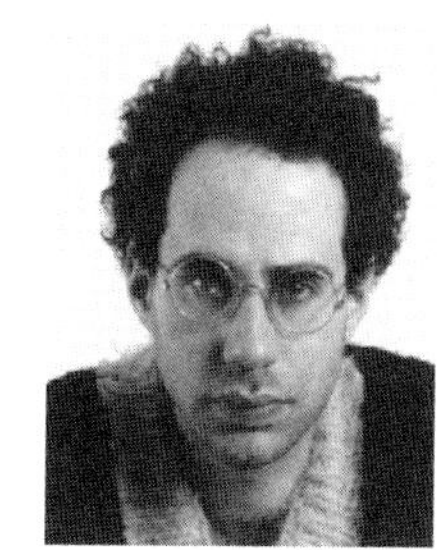

1961	*Born in Jerusalem*
1983-1986	*Studied at Bezalel Academy of Art and Design, Jerusalem*
Since 1992	*Teaches at the Kalisher School of Art, Tel Aviv*
1995	*Studied Psychology and Philosophy at Bar Ilan University*

SELECTED SOLO EXHIBITIONS (since 1985)

1994	*Dvir Gallery, Tel Aviv*
1993	*Heike Curtze Gallery, Tel Aviv*
1991	*Tel Aviv Artists' Studios*
1990	*Museum of Israeli Art, Ramat Gan (catalogue)*
1989	*Bograshov Gallery, Tel Aviv*
1988	*Mishkenot Sha'ananim, Jerusalem*
1987	*Bograshov Gallery, Tel Aviv*

SELECTED GROUP EXHIBITIONS (since 1985)

1996	*Weekly series in Cultural and Literature supplement in the newspaper "Haaretz"*
1994	*"The First Five Years," Tel Aviv Artists' Studios Homage to the Bauhaus," "I See It," Camera Obscura Gallery, Tel Aviv "Separate Worlds," Tel Aviv Museum of Art, Tel Aviv. "Anxiety," Museum of Israeli Art, Ramat Gan. Tel Hai Events*
1993	*"Makom–Comtemporary Art from Israel," Museum of Modern Art, Vienna "Antipathos-Black Humor, Irony and Cynicism in Contemporary Israeli Art," Israel Museum, Jerusalem. "Uberleben," Bonner Kunstverein, Bonn Exhibition of Winners of the Minister of Education and Culture Prize for Painting and Sculpture, Israel Museum, Jerusalem*
1992	*"Curators in Local Art," Sara Conforty Gallery, Jaffa. "Postscripts: End' Representations in Contemporary Israeli Art," The Genia Schreiber University Art Gallery, Tel Aviv University. Third Istanbul Biennale*
1991	*"Israeli Art around 1990," Stadtische Kunsthalle, Düsseldorf; Artists' House, Moscow; Israel Museum, Jerusalem. "Curators' Choice," Kalisher 5 Gallery, Tel Aviv. "Place and Mainstream - 44 From Israel - Contemporary Sculpture," Museum of Israeli Art Ramat Gan; Hara Museum, Arc, Japan; Fukuoka Art Museum 1992; National Museum of Contemporary Art, Seoul, 1992 . "Israeli Art Now - An Extensive Presentation, Summer 1991," Tel Aviv Museum of Art)*
1990	*"Tel Aviv Artists' Studios 1990." "Aperto," Venice Biennale*
1989	*The Israeli Proposal for the "Aperto," Museum of Israeli Art, Ramat Gan*
1988	*"Fresh Paint, The Younger Generation in Israeli Art," Tel Aviv Museum of Art; Israel Museum, Jerusalem; Israel Festival Jerusalem. Fortieth Anniversary of the Declaration of Human Rights, Bograshov Gallery, Tel Aviv*

PRIZES

1991	*Wolf Foundation Ingeborg Bachmann Grant founded by Anselm Kiefer*
1993	*Minister of Education and Culture Prize for Painting and Sculpture*

The fetus forced out of the womb symbolizes time before life. The fetus in formaldehyde in the Gordon House museum at Kibbutz Degania Aleph in the Jordan Valley has become part of a collective childhood memory that blends terror with curiosity. The fetal mass in the works of Daniel Sack is connected to a string as fine and strong as an umbilical cord that nourishes and binds the fetus to its mother, to another time in the life of a fertile woman, like a pendulum suspended from a taut string on a wall clock, that also has a place in memory like an object clutching foreignness, longing, and meditative monotony. The fixed route of the pendulum is the condition that assures the passage of time marking the movement of life by the clock. A small movement at the end of the string causes a wide movement of the pendulum, Just as a small change in the pregnant woman causes a big change in the fetus. The artist moves between the womb-house and the studio that extracts art from life.

Daniel Sack extends the house-studio movement and adds a psychological angle - he is intrigued, among other things, by D.W. Winnicott's discussion of the question of the transitional object and its connection to creativity.

A second definition of pendulum (Hebrew: metutellet) in the Hebrew dictionary: "a cloth (matlit), a piece of fabric hanging limp." This fabric, like the blanket, is a well known transitional object.

The object must not change, according to Winnicott, unless the infant himself changes it. It is as if Sack refuses to let the object sink into the void of oblivion and signifies it in his art works. The flower is snatched from the cloth and its place is outside, inside, and on the border.

The pouchlike blanket work is womblike, meant to carry life, but the womb has also been expropriated from the woman's body. The ascetic, rational Sack torn between flinching and pulling, exposure and concealment. From the lumpy fetuses forced from the womb a chaotic rupture develops, a kind of primeval riot that conceals beings who will never enter this world and will vanish into the edges of life. One layer is absorbed, seeps through, pours through the other. And so the layers sink into a concentrated ground, which gathers to itself with powerful sharpness the code that will never be deciphered.

Moshe Kron

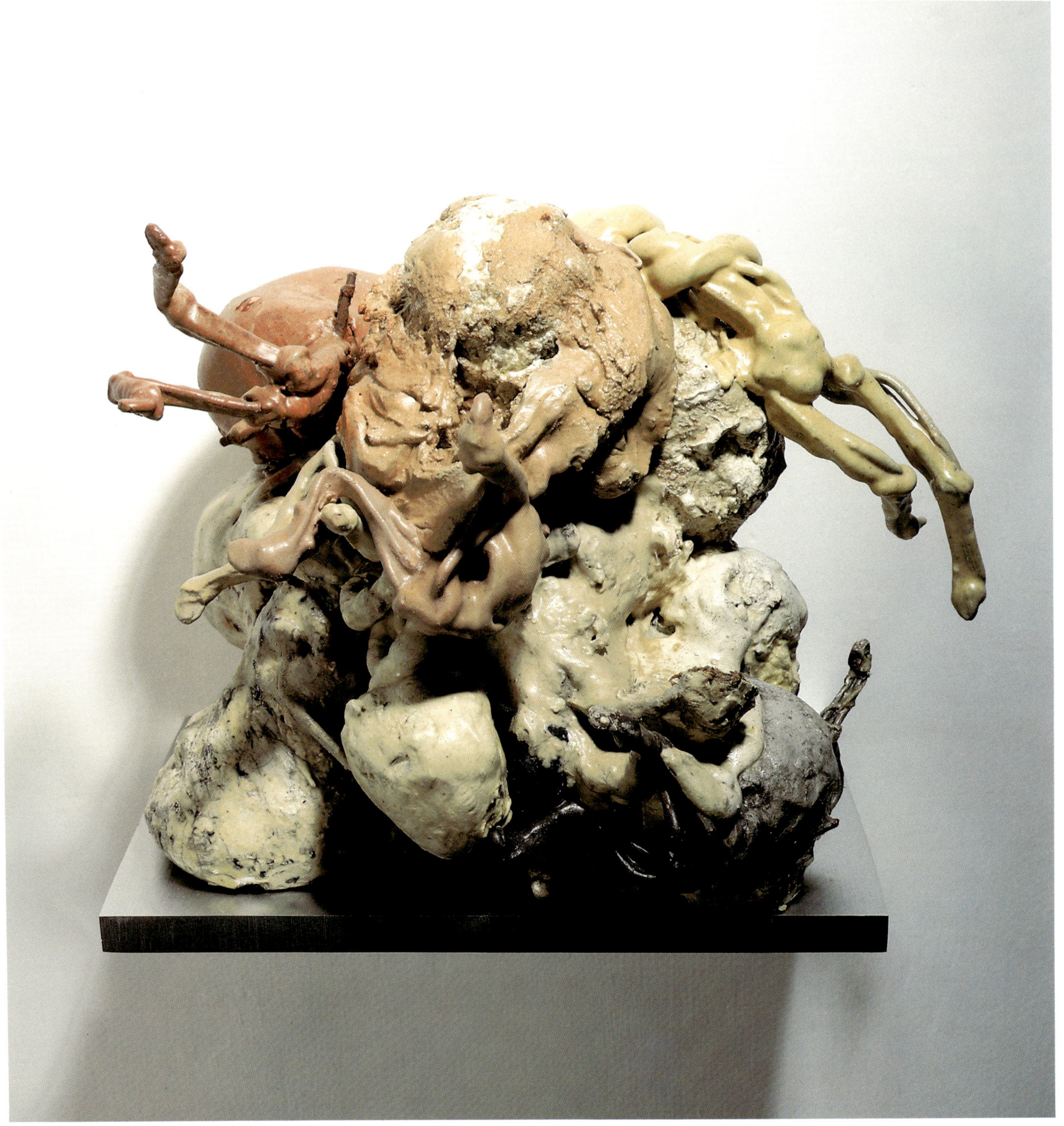

Untitled, 1992-93
ללא כותרת

Untitled, 1994
ללא כותרת

מפגש עם דניאל זק

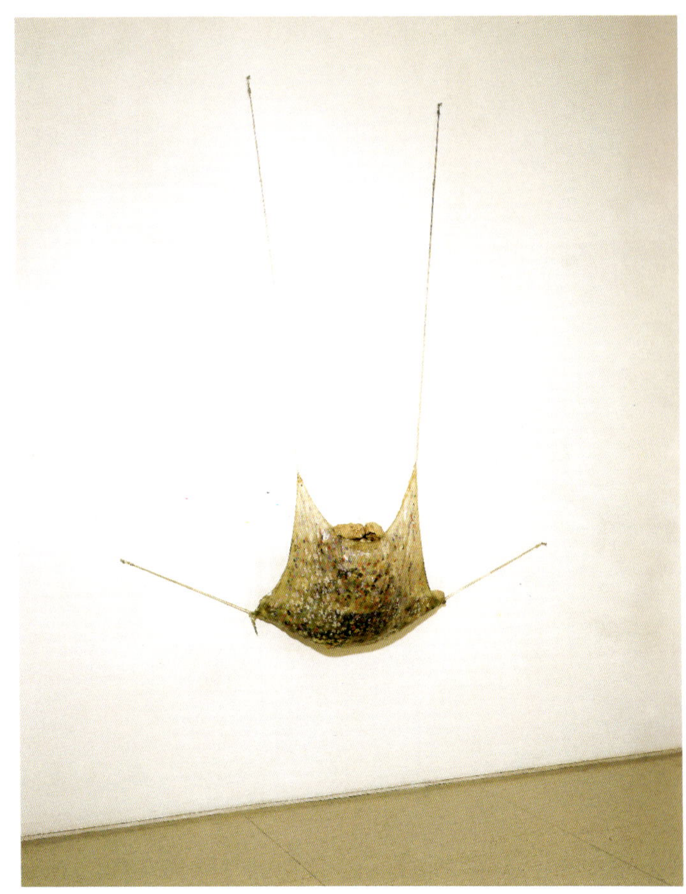

Untitled, 1993
ללא כותרת

העובר המופקע מרחם מסמן זמן שלפני ספירת החיים. העובר בצנצנת הפורמלין מבית גורדון בקבוצת דגניה א' הפך לחלק מזכרון ילדות קולקטיבי המשלב ביעות וסקרנות. הגוש העוברי בעבודות דניאל זק מחובר למיתר דק וחזק כחבל טבור המזין וקושר את העובר לאימו, לזמן אחר בחייה של אשה פוריה, כמטוטלת התלויה בקצה מיתר המתוח בתחתית שעון הקיר. שעון הקיר, שגם לו מקום בזכרון כאובייקט החופן נכר, געגועים וחדגוניות מדיטטיבית. תנועתה של המטוטלת במסלול קבוע הוא התנאי המבטיח את תנועת הזמן המסמן את תנועת החיים בשעון. תנועה קטנה בקצה המיתר גורמת לתנועה גדולה במטוטלת. כמו תמורה קטנה באם ההרה הגורמת לתמורה גדולה בעובר. האמן נע בין הבית הרחמי לבין הסטודיו המפקיע אמנות מחיים. דניאל זק מרחיב את תנועת הבית-סטודיו ומוסיף לה זווית פסיכולוגית – הוא מוקסם בין היתר מהדיון בסוגית אובייקט המעבר על-פי ד"ו ויניקוט ובהקשרו ליצירתיות. פירוש שני למטוטלת הוא של אבן-שושן : "מטלית, חתיכת-בד תלויה כמדלדלת". זו כמו הכסת הינן אובייקט מעבר נפוץ. אסור לו לאובייקט שישתנה, אומר ויניקוט, אלא אם כן התינוק עצמו משנה אותו. זק כאילו מסרב לאפשר לאובייקט לשקוע בתהום הנשייה ומסמנו בעבודותיו באמנותו. הפרח הופקע מהבד ומקומו הוא בחוץ, בפנים ועל הגבול. העבודה הכסתית הכיסית היא רחמית ואמורה לשאת חיים, אלא שגם הרחם הופקע מגוף אשה. זק הנזירי והשכלתני בניסוחיו מתחבט ברתיעות ובמשיכות, בחשיפה ובהצפנה. מהעוברים הגושיים שהופקעו מרחם מתפתחת פקעת אנדלמוסית, מעין תוהו טרום-זמני המצפין ישויות שלא יבואו לעולם ויעלמו בעיבורי החיים. שכבה נספגת, מחלחלת ונמסכת בשכבה וכך שוקעות השכבות לתוך קרקעית תמציתית המרכזת בתוכה בחריפות עזה את הצופן שלא יפוענח לעולם.

משה קרון

Mani Salama: An Encounter

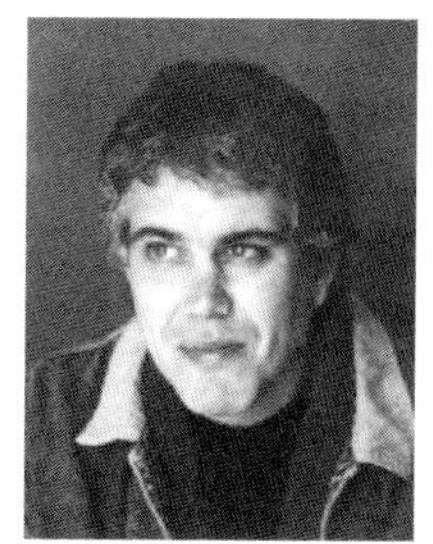

1948	*Born in Jerusalem*
	Lives and works in Jerusalem

EDUCATION

1966-68	*Studied Ceramics Department, Bezalel Academy of Art & Design, Jerusalem*

SOLO EXHIBITIONS

1994	*Kibbutz Lohamei Hagetaot*
1991	*Israel Museum, Jerusalem*
1983	*Artists House, Jerusalem*
1977	*Artists House, Jerusalem*
1975	*G.S.A. Gallery, Hilversum, Holland*
1974	*Ina Brursse Gallery, Amsterdam*
1972	*Angel Gallery, Jerusalem*

GROUP EXHIBITIONS

1995	*"An Artist Plans His Own Tombstone," Artists House, Jerusalem*
1994	*Kiryat Tivon*
1992	*Minister of Education and Culture Exhibition, Israel Museum, Jerusalem*
1986	*Artists House, Jerusalem*

PRIZES

1992	*Minister of Education and Culture Grant*
1989	*Shoshana Ish-Shalom Award*
1980	*Ofer Feniger Award*
1972	*Sharett Foundation Grant for Young Artists*
1969	*Ministry of Housing Award for a Ceramic Wall Design*

Fear does not select chance designs, in spite of appearances to the contrary. It, too, directs life's course and charges it with new logic and meaning. The art of Mani Salama is his fate, his way of dealing with the fear of death by investing it with poetry in order to survive. Part of his maturity as an artist finds expression in the resignation that follows protest.

"I move by inches," Salama says, "things move faster than I do." Mani Salama scrutinizes and works with fears, principally the fear of death, which he prefers to call "the fear of existence," the fear of vanishing memories, of the death of dear ones, of the objects that inhabit our lives.

The male sex organ that appears in Salama's work remembers that it was once a penis and remembers that it is the father of all fears. The skeleton - a symbol of death and Satan that is both simplistic and mythical - has a living mobility. From it protrudes the living male organ that occasionally evinces sparks of life. Where is the angel of death, the skeleton with the black tail? Perhaps he too is there, covered by the rhythmic scrawling in the light smoke, together with evil and malice.

The images floating in space have no hold on the ground or on reality. They appear to be clipped from a nightmare or sometimes from a sweet dream, likenesses of the boy who fell from a balcony on Jaffa Road in downtown Jerusalem and splattered to the ground, and who continues to this day to hover between earth and sky together with other children who are or who are not with us any longer, children who are also suspended in midair. Sometimes a child freezes in midair, fixing us with his piercing gaze, saying nothing.

The works, like the fears, are based on miscellanea picked up by the artist along the way: the book bindings no longer remember what books they bound; the formica or plywood surfaces no longer represent kitchen cupboards or shelves.

Mani Salama is an intimate artist who paints poetry - angelic figures, truncated either diabolically or alternatively as a reminder of romantic, childlike repose, peek out or slip from view. Delicate humor placates the beast of inner fear and tames it like the grayish cover textured like hairy skin that conceals or hides.

"When we are afraid to touch 'what is mine,' we say 'I haven't any,'" says Mani Salama, whose works stress "what is his". In the process of creation he journeys into womblike solitude; smiling ear to ear and sometimes winking mischievously or shyly, he tells the fear, and perhaps also the viewer "I haven't any".

The touchingly small format of Salama's works makes it possible to control the components of each creation and maybe also existential fear. Fear of life.

Moshe Kron

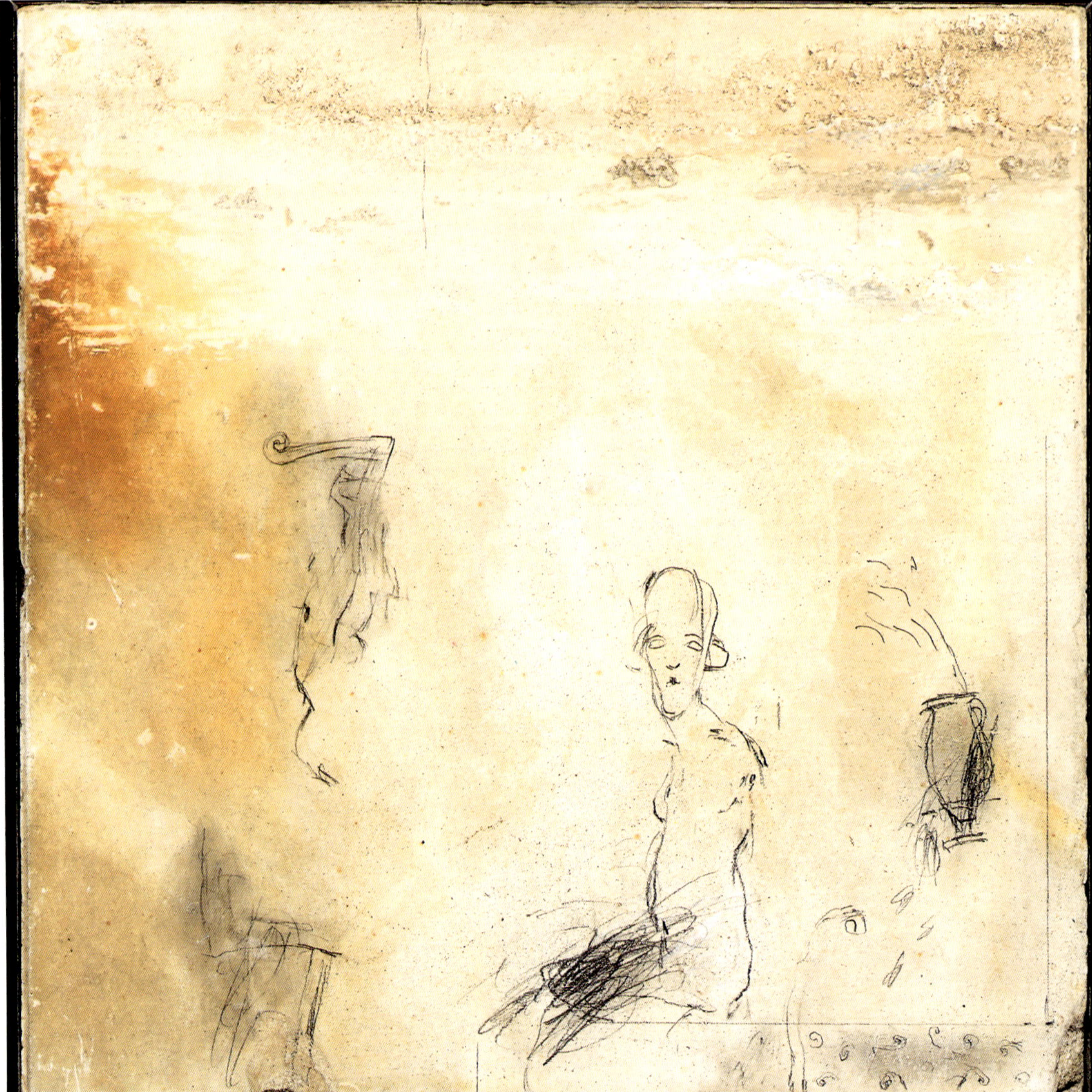

Untitled, 1996
ללא כותרת

הגיג: מני סלמה

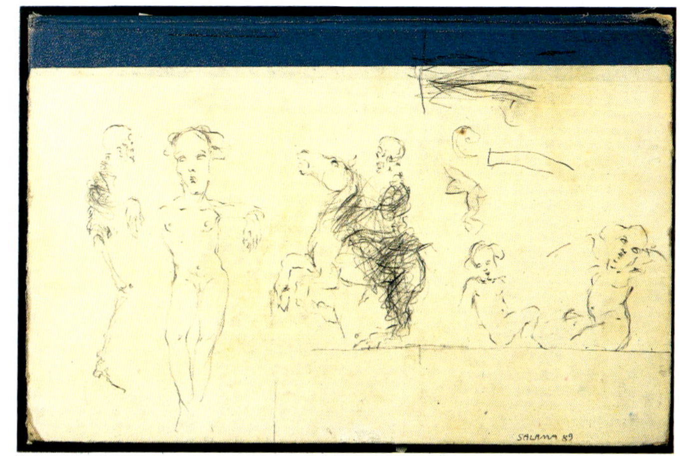

Untitled, 1989
ללא כותרת

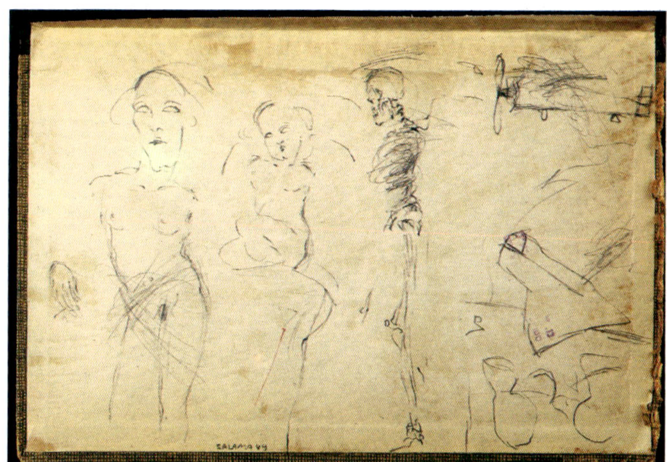

Untitled, 1989
ללא כותרת

הפחד אינו בורר לו תכנים מקריים גם אם הם נראים כך. גם הוא מכוון את החיים ויוצק לתוכם הגיון ופשר חדשים. האמנות של מני סלמה היא גורלו, זו דרכו להתמודד עם פחדי המוות, תוך חקירתם הפיוטית, ולהישרד. חלק מבגרותו כאמן באה לידי ביטוי בהשלמה הבאה בעקבות ההתרסה. "אני זז במילימטרים" מעיד סלמה על דרכו "הדברים הם אלה שזזים יותר ממני". מני סלמה מתבונן ועוסק בפחדים ובראשם בפחד המוות שהוא מעדיף לקרוא לו "פחד הקיום". פחד מהיעלמות זכרונות, ממות אנשים יקרים ומאבדן החפצים המקיפים את חיינו.

אבר המין הזכרי המופיע בעבודותיו זוכר שהיה פעם זין וזוכר שהוא אבי הפחדים. השלד-הסמל הפשטני והמיתי גם יחד למוות ולשטן, הינו בעל תנועתיות חיה, מאגנו מזדקר אבר זכרי חי שלעתים ממטיר רשפי חיות. היכן מלאך המוות – השלד שמאחוריו משחיר זנבנב? יתכן שגם הוא כוסה בשירבוט הקצבי בעשן הבהיר יחד עם הרוע והרשע.

הדמויות המרחפות בחלל אין להן אחיזה בקרקע במציאות. הן גזורות כמו מתוך חלום ביעותים, או לרגעים - חלום מתוק. בנות דמותו של ילד שנפל ממרפסת ביתו ברחוב יפו במרכז ירושלים ונחבט בקרקע, וממשיך לרחף עד היום בין שמים לארץ, עם עוד ילדים שישנם ואינם עוד בינינו, ילדים המרחפים גם הם בין לבין. לפעמים עומד לו ילד ללא נוע באוויר, מתבונן בנו בעיניו הנוקבות ואינו אומר דבר.

העבודות מתבייתות כמו הפחדים על חומרים הנקרים בדרכו של האמן : כריכות הספרים אינן זוכרות עוד את הספר ומשטחי הפורמיקה או הדיקט אינם מייצגים עוד את ארונות המטבח או המדפים. מני סלמה הוא אמן אינטימי המצייר שירה. הדמויות המלאכיות הקטועות כמעשה שטן או לחילופין כאיזכור לשכבה ילדית רומנטית, צצות ומסתתרות. ההומור המעודן בא לרצות את חית הפחד הפנימי ולשלוט בה כמו הכיסוי האפור בעל המרקם העורי השעיר המחביא או מתחבא. "כשפוחדים לגעת ב'שלי' אומרים 'אין לי' " אומר מני סלמה העסוק בעבודותיו ב'שלו'. בתהליך עיבוד התכנים הוא מתכנס ומתרחק לתוך בדידות רחמית, בחיוך מלא המלווה לעתים בקריצה שובבית ומבוישת הוא אומר לפחד, ואולי גם לצופה, "אין לי".

הפורמט הקטן, שיש בו צניעות מעוררת כבוד, הוא המעניק את יכולת השליטה על תכנים ואולי גם את הפיקוח על פחד הקיום. על החיים.

משה קרון

Micha Ullman: An Interview

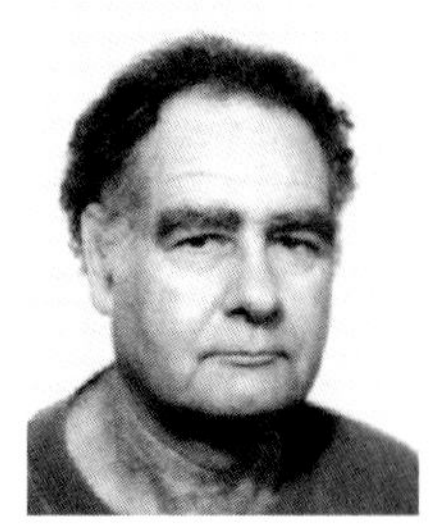

1939	*Born in Tel Aviv*
1960-64	*Studied at the Bezalel Academy of Art and Design, Jerusalem*
1965	*Studied at the Central School for Arts and Crafts, London*
1970-78	*Taught drawing and basic design and etching at the Bezalel Academy of Art and Design, Jerusalem*
1976	*Guest Teacher at the Hochschule for Bildende Kurnste, Düsseldorf*
1979	*Taught sculpture and drawing at the Fine Arts Department, Haifa University*
1985	*Sabbatical in New York*
1989	*DAAD - Stipendium, Berlin*
1991	*Professor at the Akadamie der Bildenden Kunste, Stuttgart*
	Lives in Ramat Hasharon, Israel

SELECTED SOLO EXHIBITIONS (since 1985)

1996	*Drawings 1994-1995, Tel Aviv Museum of Art*
1995	*"Monat" Zeichnungen, Galerie Cora Holzl, Düsseldorf*
	Exhibition on the occasion of the Kathe Kollwitz Prize, Akademie der Kunste, Berlin
1994	*"Halal - Arte Contemporanea da Israele," Galeria 5-55, Rome*
	"Neumond," Bodenskulptur und "Monat" Zeichnungen, Akademie Schloss Solitude, Stuttgart
1993	*Het Apollohuis, Eindhoven*
	Givon Art Gallery, Tel Aviv
1992	*Europaisches Kulturzentrum in Thuringen, Erfurt, Germany*
	Gallery Yamaguchi, Osaka
1990	*Galerie Cora Holzl, Düsseldorf*
1989	*20th Sao Paulo International Biennial (with Danny Shoshan)*
1988	*Israel Museum, Jerusalem*
1987	*Galerie Cora Holzl, Düsseldorf*
1986	*Bertha Urdang Gallery, New York*

SELECTED GROUP EXHIBITIONS (Since 1985)

1995	*"Co-existence," Construction In Process, Mizpe Rimon, Israel*
	"Where is Abel, Thy Brother," National Gallery of Contemporary Art, Warsaw
	Observation Fredsskulptor Atlantikwall, Jutland, Denmark
	Köln Art Fair, Galerie Cora Holzl, Düsseldorf
	"Orientation," Istanbul Biennale 4
	"Interventions," Museo de las Bellas Artes, Caracas, Venezuela
1994	*Funfter Mai Salon, Kunst in Berlin, Ern Neuen Kunstquartier Berlin*
	"Along New Lines: Israeli Drawings Today," Israel Museum, Jerusalem
	"Emphasis," Israel Museum, Jerusalem
	Basel Art Fair, Givon Gallery, Tel Aviv
	Art Focus, "Israeli Sculpture in Tefen, The Last Decade," Open Museum, Industrial Park, Tefen
1993	*"Makom," Museum modemer Kunst, Palais Liechtenstein, Vienna*

Since the seventies Micha Ullman has been producing conceptual art related to the earth. Previously he made etchings, which are a form of digging into the copper plate.

At first he made symbolic attempts at politically unifying the two peoples inhabiting the State of Israel, Jews and Arabs. He dug pits in Kibbutz Metzer and in the Arab village of Messer. He filled the pits in the kibbutz with earth from the village and those in the village with earth from the kibbutz. Youngsters from the Arab village and kibbutz members helped him with this work.

The "earth" work represents people's primordial attachment to their origins, to nature and the universe: "And the Lord God formed man of the dust of the ground, and breathed into his nostrils the breath of life; and man became a living soul." (**Genesis** 2:7)

Digging is our connection to our origins. We dig in order to know the earth, to discover and understand the history of a place; we dig to fertilize the earth, to plant and sow, to produce food; we dig to hide during war and to return the dead to their ancestors: "For out of it wast thou taken: for dust thou are, and unto dust shalt thou return." (**Genesis** 3:19)

NC: Many of your works are under the ground, sometimes with only a partial detail visible on the surface. One can walk by without even noticing them.

MU: This is a language of clues. In many cases my works are hardly visible, and the viewer has only minimal information about them. This may be a rusty iron piece that could be taken for an archaeological detail cropping out through the earth. Over time, even this clue may be covered with another layer of earth or weeds in addition to the grass I originally planted. Like the work at the eighth Documenta in Kassel.

NC: You actually invite the viewer to act?

MU: Yes, I think that the clue, the work's visible part, allows the viewer to actively participate. In this sense there is an invitation to act and take a stand. However, the work doesn't impose itself on the viewer and doesn't force him to do anything. Only if he is interested is he invited to search, "dig," that is, to discover the work.

House, 1993
בית

1992	*"Place & Mainstream," Israel Contemporary Sculpture, Fukuoka Art Museum, Japan*
	National Museum for Contemporary Art, Korea
	"Routes of Wandering," Israel Museum, Jerusalem
	Documenta 9, Kassel
1991	*"Dez Artistas de Israel," Museum de Arte de Sao Paolo*
	"Museum und Kirche, Wilhem-Lehmbruck-Museum, Duisburg, Germany
	"Stein und Orteî Stadisches Museum, Schloss Morsbroich, Leverkusen, Germany
	"Place & Mainstream," Museum of Israeli Art, Ramat Gan
	"The Presence of the Absent," University Art Gallery, Tel Aviv
	"Israel Contemporary Sculpture" (traveling exhibition), Hara Museum, ARC, Gunma, Japan
	"Sculptures," Gallery Yamaguchi, Osaka, Japan
	"Israeli Art Around 1990," Kunsthalle, Düsseldorf; Moscow, Jerusalem
	"Works on Paper," Tel Aviv Workshops
1990	*"Europaische Skulptur der Zeiten Moderne," Lehmbruck Museum, Durisburg, Germany*
	"Construction in Process, Back in Lodz," Lodz, Poland
	"Chagall to Kitaj," Barbican Art Gallery, London
1989	*"In the Shadow of Conflict," Jewish Museum, New York*
1987	*Documenta 8, Kassel1986: "The Disciplined Spirit," Exit Art Gallery, New York*
	Art Park, Lewiston, New York
	"Skulpersein," Kunsthalle, Düsseldorf
1985	*"1983-1984: Two Years of Israeli Art - Qualities Accumulated," Tel Aviv Museum of Art*
	Contemporary Art Meeting, Tel Hai

PUBLIC SPACE SCUPTURES

1995	*Bibliotek, Bebelplatz, Berlin*
	Observation, Fredsskulptur, Atlantik Wall, Jutland, Denmark
	Gate, Performing Arts Center, Tel Aviv
	Glass House, Museo de las Bellas Artes, Caracas, Venezuela
1994	*Nemtond, Akademie Schloss Solitude, Stuttgart*
1992	*Sea Level, 22 Allenby St., Tel Aviv*
	Niemand, Gropius Bau, Berlin
1991	*Scholdnia (East), Lodz, Poland*
1990	*Waage, Neuenkirchen, Germany*
1988	*Sitting, Golda Park, Ramle, Israel*
1986	*Equation, Kunsthalle, Düsseldorf*
1984	*Lot's Wife, Mt. Sodom, Israel*
1983	*Sky, Tel Hai, Israel*
1980	*Mirror, Tel Aviv Museum of Art*

NC: So you don't mind if a large number of potential viewers won't even know that your work is there?

MU: There is a question here, or a riddle. The invisible is more important than the visible, because the viewer directs the invisible to channels that interest him and to associations close to him. One person may see the work as an iceberg almost entirely sunk in water, another may venture into archaeological layers to find out what they hide. Still another may think about the graves of ancestors or relatives.

NC: Which means that the minimal information you provide allows for any interpretation, which reminds me of the possibilities implicit in "Bibliotheka," your Berlin work. [It deals with book burning by the Nazis in the thirties. It is built underground like a transparent library room. The room's four glass walls are lined with empty bookshelves. Above ground is a square window through which the viewer can look down into the lighted library without books.]

MU: "Bibliotheka" is a German word whose sound is reminiscent of Bible and Babylon. Again the viewer is invited to discover the invisible. Of course, the transparent window may be covered with sand, dust, earth, mud, rain, and the visitor's footprints. In any case the viewer must be sufficiently curious in order to stop and find out what he sees underneath him. That's when he can open up to the possibilities implicit in the work's title. Each viewer can add his own connotations to the existing interpretations.

NC: Your work is set up in open spaces and people and nature can change them to some extent.

MU: I've taken this into consideration. Some changes occur naturally, over time. Iron, for example, oxidizes and rusts and its color comes closer and closer to the color of the earth. I find the change over time interesting . . . In the 1990 works in Düsseldorf I placed sand in boxes. The sand actually worked like a seismograph. When there was a tremor, it was immediately "registered," because sand is a sensitive material that registers every movement, whether natural or man induced. What happens with sand happens with iron and rust.

Nella Cassouto

AWARDS

1996 *Sussmann Prize, Yad Vashem, Jerusalem*
1995 *Kathe Kollwitz Prize, Akademie der Kunste, Berlin*
1985 *Tel Aviv Museum of Art Mendel and Eva Pundik Prize for Israeli Art*
1980 *Israel Museum's Sandberg Prize for an Israeli Artist*
1972 *Israel Museum's Beatrice S. Kolliner Prize for a Young Israeli Artist*
1963 *Someborn Prize of the Bezalel Academy of Art and Design, Jerusalem*

THERE WAS EARTH INSIDE THEM, and they dug.

They dug and they dug, so their day
went by for them, their night. And they did not praise
God.
who, so they heard, wanted all this,
who, so they heard, knew all this.

They dug and heard nothing more;
they did not grow wise, invented no song,
thought up for themselves no language.
They dug.

There came a stillness, and there came a storm,
and all the oceans came.
I dig, you dig, and the worm digs too,
and that singing out there says: They dig.

On one, o none, o no one, o you:
Where did the way lead when it led nowhere?
O you dig and I dig, and I dig towards you,
and on our finger the ring awakes.

Poems
Paul Celan
trans. Michael Hamburger
Persea Books, New York, 1980
p. 131

אדמה היתה בהם, והם חפרו

הם חפרו וחפרו, כך עבר
עליהם יומם, לילם. ולא הללו את אלהים,
ששמעו כי רצה בכל זה,
ששמעו כי ידע על כל זה.

הם חפרו ושוב לא שמעו דבר;
לא החכימו, לא המציאו שיר,
לא תכנו להם שפה.
הם חפרו.

ובאה דממה, גם סופה באה,
ובאו כל הימים.
אני חופר, את חופרת, וחופרת התולעת,
והשר שם אומר: הם חופרים.

הו איש, הו שום-איש, הו לא-איש, הו את:
לאן הלך מה שאבד?
את חופרת ואני מתחפר עדיך
וטבעת מקיצה על היד.

פאול צלאן, **סורג-שפה**
מגרמנית: שמעון זנדבנק,
ירושלים 1995, עמ' 45.

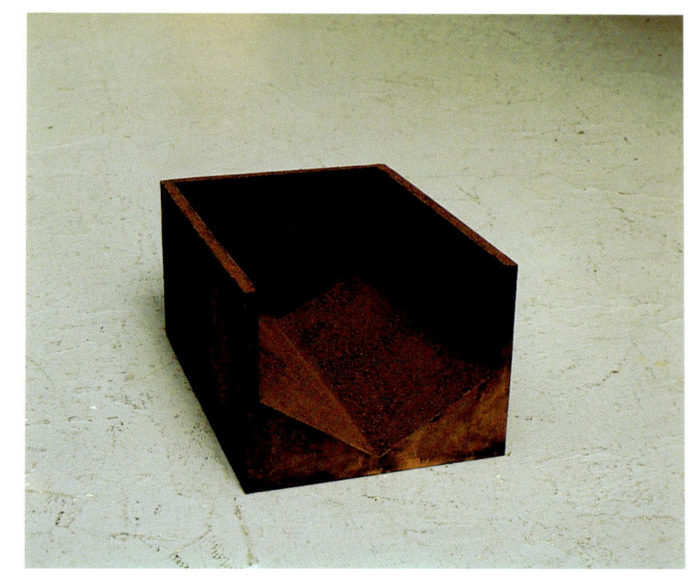

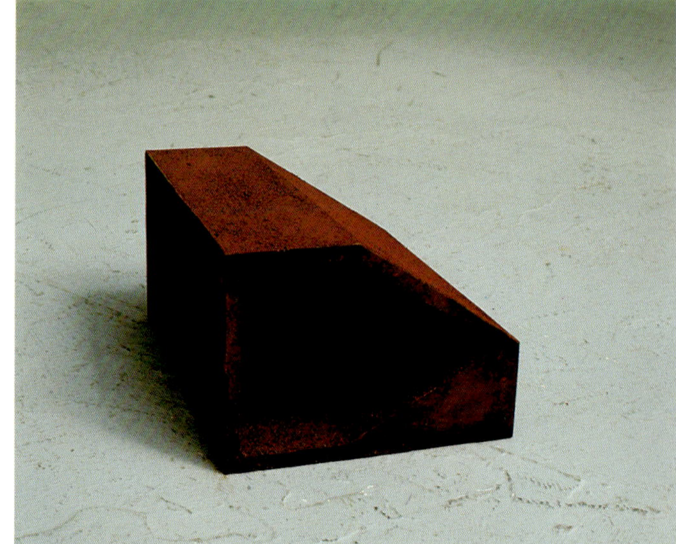

נ"ק: כלומר, המידע המינימלי שאתה נותן מאפשר כל אינטרפרטציה, דבר המזכיר את האפשרויות הגלומות ביצירתך "ביבליותיקה" הנמצאת בברלין.

העבודה מטפלת בנושא שריפת ספרים (בידי הנאצים, בשנות השלושים). היא בנויה מתחת לפני הקרקע, בצורת חדר ספרייה שקוף. ממדי החדר – 5.29 X 7.06 X 7.06 מ' – אלו מידות שנקבעו על פי גבהו של האמן כפול 4, ועל פי רחבו המוכפל פי 3.

על ארבעת קירות הזכוכית מדפי ספרים ריקים. מעל פני הקרקע חלון זכוכית מרובע (1.20 X 1.20 מ') שדרכו יכול הצופה להביט כלפי מטה ולראות את הספרייה המוארת שאין בה ספרים.

מ"א: "ביבליותיקה" (Bibliothek) היא מלה גרמנית שצלילה מזכיר את המלה Bible (תנ"ך) ואת המלה בבל. אך שוב, הצופה מוזמן לגלות את הבלתי-נראה. מובן שהחלון השקוף המאפשר לצופה להביט למטה ופנימה יכול להתכסות בחול, אבק, אדמה, בוץ, גשם ועקבות רגליהם של המבקרים.

על כל פנים, על המבקר להיות סקרן דיו כדי שיעצור ויחפש מה נמצא מתחתיו. רק אז הוא פתוח לאפשרויות הגלומות בכותרת העבודה. כל צופה יכול להוסיף לפירוש הקיים פירוש נוסף הנלקח מתחום ההקשרים הפרטיים שלו.

נ"ק: עבודותיך משובצות במרחב הפתוח ולכן האנשים והטבע יכולים לשנותם במשהו.

מ"א: התחשבתי בכך. שינויים מסוימים קורים באופן טבעי, במהלך הזמן. ברזל, לדוגמא, עובר תהליך חימצון ומחליד, ואז הופך צבעו יותר ויותר קרוב לצבע האדמה. השינוי הקורה בזמן מעניין לדעתי...

בעבודותי משנת 1990 שעשיתי בדיסלדורף מלאתי ארגזי עץ בחול. למעשה פעל החול כמו סייסמוגרף. כאשר היתה רעידה, היא "נרשמה" מיד, כיוון שחול הינו חומר רגיש הרושם כל תנודה, ותהא טבעית או מעשה ידי אדם. מה שקורה לחול דומה למה שקורה לברזל ולחלודה.

נלה קסוטו

מיכה אולמן

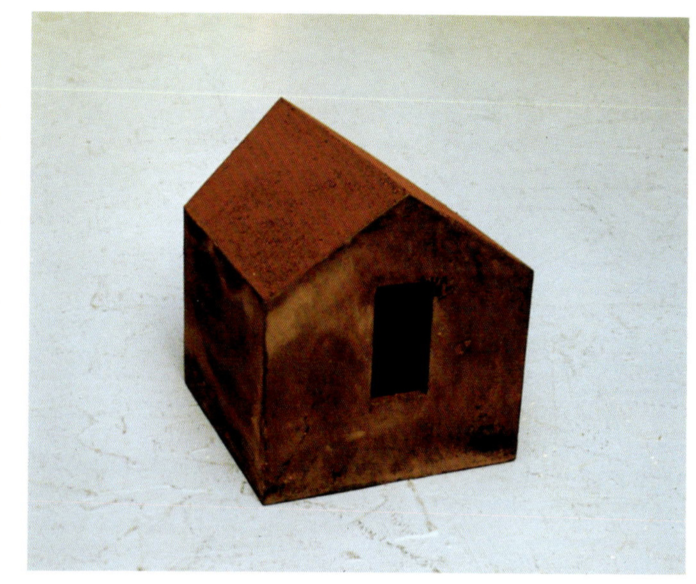

Midnight, 1990
חצות

Day, 1990
יום

Havdala, 1990
הבדלה

מאז שנות השבעים יצר מיכה אולמן יצירות אמנות קונספטואליות הקשורות לאדמה. לפני כן עשה תחריטים – צורה של חפירה לתוך יריעת הנחושת.

תחילה עשה ניסיון לאחד מבחינה פוליטית את שני העמים היושבים במדינת ישראל, את היהודים והערבים. הוא חפר בורות בקבוץ מצר ובכפר הערבי מסר. את הבורות שחפר בקבוץ מילא באדמת הכפר ואת הבורות שחפר בכפר מילא באדמת הקבוץ.

צעירים מן הכפר הערבי ומן הקבוץ עזרו לו במלאכתו זו.

עבודת "האדמה" מייצגת את הקשר הראשוני של עמים למקורותיהם, לטבע וליקום.

"וייצר יהוה אלהים את האדם עפר מן האדמה ויפח באפיו נשמת חיים, ויהי האדם לנפש חיה" (**בראשית**, ב:7)
החפירה הינה הקשר הקושר אותנו למקורותינו. אנו חופרים כדי להכיר את האדמה, כדי לגלות ולהבין את תולדותיו של מקום; אנו חופרים כדי להפרות את האדמה, כדי לחרוש ולנטוע, לייצר מזון; אנו חופרים כדי להסתתר בזמן מלחמה וכדי להשיב את המתים לאבותיהם: "בזעת אפיך תאכל לחם עד שובך אל האדמה כי ממנה לקחת, כי עפר אתה ואל עפר תשוב"
(**בראשית**, ג:19)

נלה קסוטו: רבות מיצירותיך מצויות מתחת לפני הקרקע, פעמים רק חלק קטן בולט על פני השטח. אפשר לעבור לידן מבלי להבחין בהן.

מיכה אולמן: זוהי אכן שפת רמזים. במקרים רבים יצירותי כמעט בלתי נראות, ולמסתכל מידע מזערי עליהן. זו יכולה להיות חתיכת ברזל חלודה שאפשר לחשבה לשריד ארכאולוגי הבולט מעל פני הקרקע. במשך הזמן אפילו רמז זה עלול להתכסות בשכבות אדמה ועשבים הנוספים על הדשא שאני עצמי שתלתי, כמו היצירה בדוקומטה השמינית בקאסל.

נ"ק: האם אתה מזמין את הצופה לפעול?

מ"א: כן, אני חושב שהרמז, החלק הבולט לעין של היצירה, מתיר לצופה לפעול. במובן זה ישנה הזמנה לפעול ולנקוט עמדה. אבל היצירה איננה מכריחה את הצופה לעשות משהו. הוא פועל רק אם הוא מעוניין בכך, הוא "חופר", כלומר, מגלה את העבודה.

נ"ק: פירוש הדבר שלא אכפת לך אם חלק מן הצופים הפוטנציאליים לא יבחינו ביצירתך כלל?

מ"א: מתעוררת שאלה, או אולי חידה. הבלתי נראה חשוב מן הנראה, כיוון שהצופה מכוון את הבלתי נראה למה שמעניין אותו ולהקשרים הקרובים ללבו.

צופה אחד יכול לראות בעבודה קרחון השקוע כמעט כולו במים, ואחר ינסה לחדור לשכבות ארכאולוגיות כדי לגלות מה מסתתר בהן. ואחר יחשוב אולי על קברי אבותיו או קרוביו.

Morphology of Memory: The Art of Yocheved Weinfeld

1947 Born in Legnica, Poland
1957 Immigrated to Israel
1981 Lives in the U.S.A.

EDUCATION

1979-80 Film and Video at the New School For Social Research
1977 M.F.A, University of Capetown
1970 B.A, The Hebrew University, Jerusalem
1967 Art Teaching Diploma, State Art Teaching College, Tel Aviv

SELECTED SOLO EXHIBITIONS

1991 Bograshov Gallery, Tel Aviv
1982 Gordon Gallery, Tel Aviv
1981 Gordon Gallery, Tel Aviv

SELECTED GROUP EXHIBITIONS (from 1980)

1992 "Goodbye to Apple Pie," De Cordova Museum, Lincoln Ma.
"9 Artists' Social Views," J. Claremont Gallery, N.Y.
1991 "Hastings-on-Hudson," N.Y.
1987 "Archetype/Symbol/Photograph," O Roe Electric Art Space, Hoboken,
1985 "Four Walls," Hoboken, N.Y.
1984 The University Art Gallery, State University at Albany, N.Y.
1983 The Ritz Show, (organized by Colab), Ritz Hotel
1981 "Trends in Israeli Art 1970-81," Basel Art Fair, Basel
"Ung Kunst fra Israel," Henie Onstaad Kunstsenter, Hovlkoden, Norway
"Artists From Israel," Jewish Museum, New York

The art of Yocheved Weinfeld is loaded with echoes and traces of the past. The works she has created over the last two decades are composed of words and images that reconstruct the morphology of her layered memories. Collecting and re-collecting fragments of her past, voices remembered from childhood, faded images of real and imagined emotional memories — Weinfeld pieces together stories and histories.

Weinfeld was born in post World War II Poland to parents who were Holocaust survivors. Although they rarely talked about their wartime experiences, the burden of their untold memories and traumas dominated the artist's world as a child. As an adult, her art taps a haunted space where her own personal experiences – filtered through the prism of memory – merge with the images suggested by her parents' ominous silence.

In a 1979 one-woman show at the Israel Museum, Weinfeld exhibited ten large, horizontal, complex mixed-media works composed of a written text and visual images. In each text — a first-person narrative that reconstructs the voice of the artist as a little girl – a powerful experience from early childhood is told. These memories often relate to anti-Semitism, sexuality, and stories of the Holocaust.

The commandant's son was sitting in the avenue on a bench. His hair was yellow. When I came near he said dirty Jew, opened his trousers and pissed on my legs.

Kazia and I are standing on the wooden veranda. Kazia sends me to buy cigarettes. Afterwards she gives me a puff and says, there was a girl in our village who played with a wooden stick between her legs and then blood came out I bleed from there every month. If a girl is pregnant a yellow juice comes out.

In the concentration camps where all the Jews were dirty and hungry there were also beautiful women whom the Germans loved. So the women would beat Jews and get food. Now they are being punished. Their heads were shaven.

Diverse visual images are linked to each nodal childhood episode, like clusters of grapes on a vine. Some represent faded memories and are visualized as vague abstract compositions or as grainy black-and-white photographs; others are sharp-edged, colorful and clearly focused presenting images that are vividly remembered.

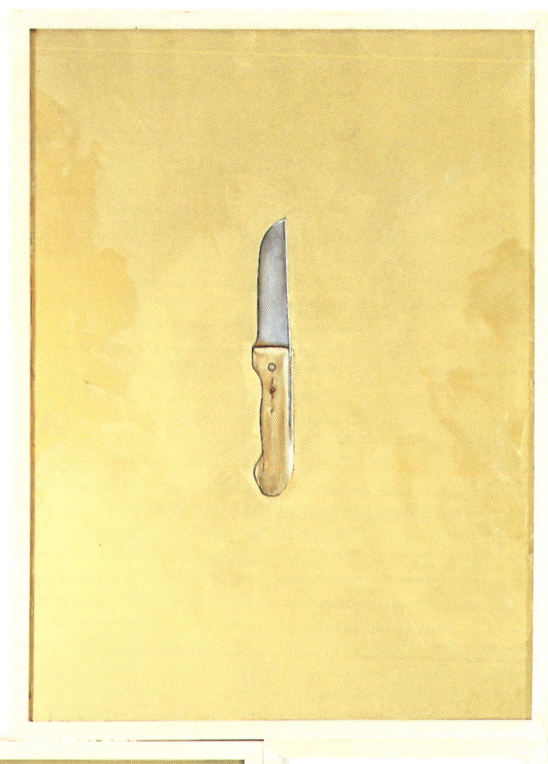

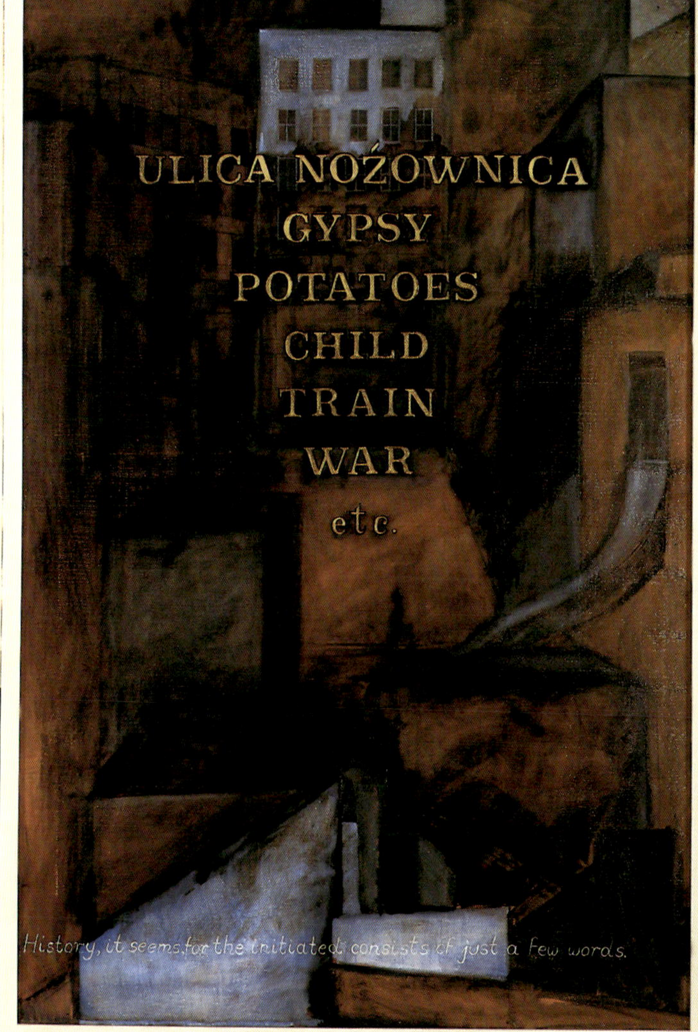

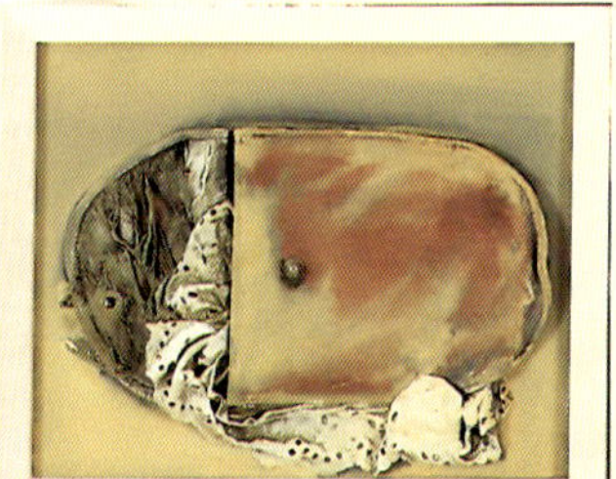

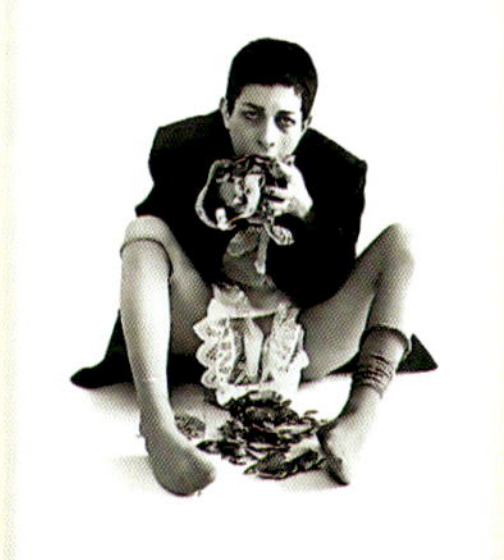

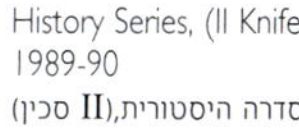

History Series, (II Knife),
1989-90
סדרה היסטורית,(סכין II)

In 1981 Weinfeld created a series based on memories of stories that her mother told her over and over again when she was a child.

Eat eat, in the war people even ate potato peels.

You have to be very careful. One night lice dragged a girl from her bed into the forest.

You must always wear clean underwear. You might be killed in an accident and then what . . .

The voice of the mother telling her tales stirred the child's imagination. The artist remembers the potent images. As she transforms them into visual art, she recreates and thus exorcises the child's fears and traumas.

The series shown in this exhibition is composed of five works created in 1989-1990. The texts included in each work speak in two different voices:

A general text, which gives the series its name, is written at the bottom of each work and relates a rational theoretical statement:

"History, it seems, for the initiated, consists of just a few words."

The "few words" of the title are spoken in a different voice. Like a Freudian free-association session, they move backward in time, uncovering layered memories that lead back to that inevitable abyss, war.

forest, wolf, milk, child, train, war, etc.

snow, coal, razor, skull, train, war, etc.

home, dunes, fish, thighs, war, etc.

garden, eve, ball, child, camp, war, etc.

ulica nozownica, gypsy, potatoes, child, train, war, etc.

"The initiated" share a collective memory. They are doomed by memory. They cannot think of a train without seeing Auschwitz; they cannot think of a shaven head or a striped shirt without visualizing the camps. More disturbingly, they cannot think of a child, of the color yellow, or of a ball without their chain of thoughts leading into darkness.

Weinfeld adds the word "etc." with its ironic matter-of-fact quality to her list of words. Thus "etc." substitutes for the most profound childhood memories, the burden of repressed stories, sensed but never uttered, imagined but never explicitly told.

Words trigger emotional memories from childhood. Memories carry with them clusters of loaded images. Like dust balls in the desert, Weinfeld's memories roll on and on, accumulating discarded matter, energized by the wind, growing, disappearing, reappearing; always moving in unexpected directions.

Gannit Ankori

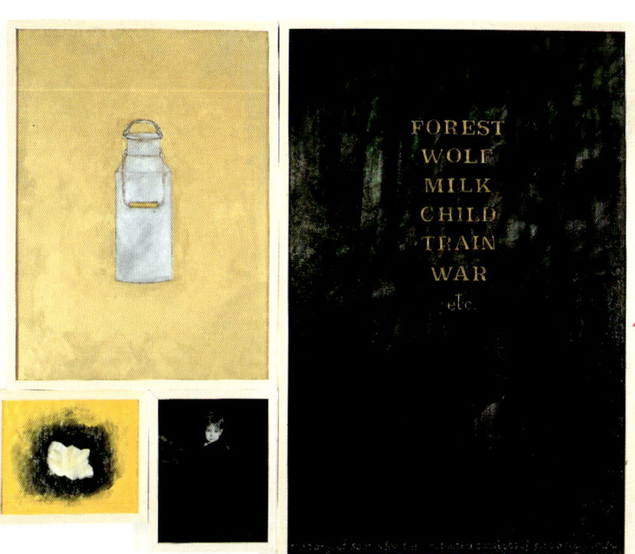

History Series, (I Milk),
1989-90
סדרה היסטורית,(I חלב)

הסדרה המוצגת בתערוכה הנוכחית מורכבת מחמש עבודות שנוצרו בשנים 1989-1990. הטקסטים, המהווים חלק אינטגראלי של כל יצירה, מדברים בשני קולות נבדלים:

הטקסט הכללי, הנותן לסידרה את שמה, כתוב בתחתית כל עבודה ומהווה הצהרה תיאורטית רציונאלית: *"history, it seems, for the initiated, consists of just a few words".*

הטקסט כתוב בשפה האנגלית, שפת ארץ מגוריה הנוכחית של וינפלד. "המלים הספורות" שמהן מורכבת ההיסטוריה נהגות בקול אחר, קול אישי המזרים מלים ב"זרם תודעה" והממזג בין הפרטי, האסוציאטיבי לבין ההיסטורי הקולקטיבי.

יער, זאב, חלב, ילד, רכבת, מלחמה, וכו'

שלג, פחם, תער, גולגולת, רכבת, מלחמה, וכו'

בית, דיונות, דגים, ירכיים, מלחמה, וכו'

גן, חוה, כדור, ילד, מחנה, מלחמה, וכו'

Ulica Nozownica, צועני, תפוחי אדמה, ילד, רכבת, מלחמה, וכו'

הסדרה – על מרכיביה המילוליים והחזותיים – מותחת קו בין נאראטיב אישי לבין נאראטיב כללי, ומקשרת בין הקול הרציונאלי, המצביע על נקודת ההשקה בין הלינגויסטיקה וההיסטוריה לבין הקול הפרטי, המדגים מקרה ספציפי של עקרון זה.

"יודעי הדבר" – הנתונים בסוד העניינים (the initiated) אינם חברי כת סודית, אלא שותפים בעל כורחם לעול הזכרון הקולקטיבי. הם כבולים לשרשרת תגובות המקשרת באופן בלתי נמנע ובלתי נשלט בין כל איזכור לבין תהום אפלה. מלים טעונות (רכבת, ראש מגולח, כתונת פסים) ומלים תמימות לכאורה (ילד, צהוב, כדור) מציתות תבנית חשיבה המובילה לזכרון המלחמה והאבדן.

מלים מעוררות זכרונות. הזכרונות מתעבים לדימויים. הדימויים נערמים ברבדי התודעה והזכרון. וינפלד חושפת ערימות של דימויים, מפרקת זכרונות ומרכיבה אותם מחדש. עקבות תהליכי ההמשגה וההמחשה של תהליך ההדחקה, ההיזכרות ונצירת הזכרון נחשפים באמנותה, המשחזרת את המורפולוגיה של הזכרון.

גנית אנקורי

המורפולוגיה של הזכרון
אמנותה של יוכבד וינפלד

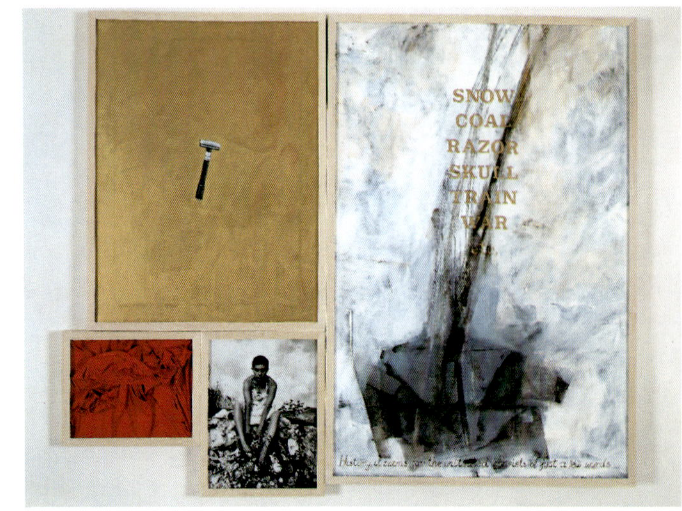

History Series, (III Razor), 1989-90
סדרה היסטורית,(III סכין גלוח)

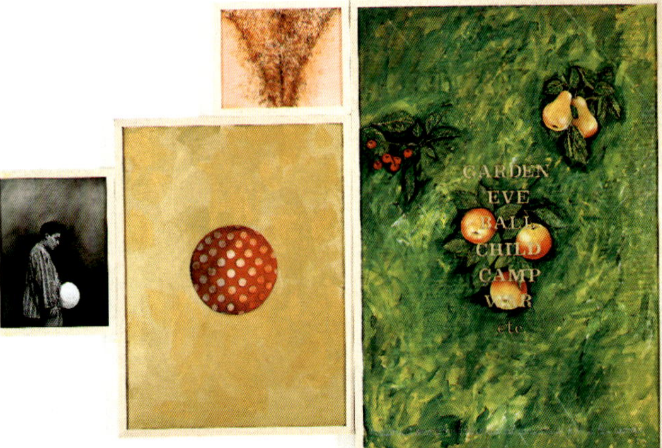

History Series, (IV Ball)), 1989-90
סדרה היסטורית,(IV כדור)

קולות מן העבר מהדהדים באמנותה של יוכבד וינפלד. קרעי דמיון ומציאות, צלילי ילדות, ודמויים מעורפלים או חדי-מיתאר מתלכדים ביצירותיה ומשחזרים מורפולוגיה של זכרון רב-רבדים.

עבודותיה של וינפלד נוגעות במרווחים שבין השתיקות של הוריה, ניצולי השואה, ובחוויות ילדות, שנתעצבו בצל עבר מעיק, המתגבש מחדש דרך מנסרת ההיזכרות.

ב-1979 במסגרת תערוכת יחיד במוזיאון ישראל, הציגה וינפלד מספר עבודות המורכבות מטקסט ומדימויים חזותיים הכרוכים בו. הטקסט מדבר בקולה של האמנית – כילדה המספרת בגוף ראשון חוויית ילדות שנחרטה בזכרון.

הבן של מפקד המשטרה ישב בשדרה על ספסל. היו לו שערות צהובות. כשהתקרבתי אמר יהודיה מלוכלכת פתח את מכנסיו והשתין על רגלי.

קז'יה ואני עומדות על מרפסת העץ. קז'יה שולחת אותי לקנות סיגריות. אחר-כך היא נותנת לי מציצה ואומרת אצלנו בכפר היתה בחורה אחת ששיחקה עם מקל בין הרגלים אחר-כך ירד לה דם אצלי כל חודש יורד דם משם. אם בחורה בהריון יוצא לה מיץ צהוב.

במחנות הריכוז שבהם היו כל היהודים מלוכלכים ורעבים היו גם נשים יפות שהגרמנים אהבו. אז הן הרביצו ליהודים וקבלו אוכל. עכשיו מענישים אותן. היו להן ראשים מגולחים.

החוויות, המדווחות בשפה ישירה בטקסטים, קשורות בתחושות השפלה ומבוכה, בתהליכי התבגרות ובגיבוש זהות אישית, מינית ולאומית. הדימויים החזותיים שמעורר כל זכרון מתלכדים סביבו, חושפים, מפרקים ומרכיבים מחדש את רבדי התודעה העצמית.

ב-1981 יצרה וינפלד סדרת עבודות המבוססת על סיפורים שסיפרה לה אמה, פעם אחר פעם. קולה של האם, כפי שהוא נטמן בזכרון בתה והדימויים שהוא מעורר, מחליף את קול הילדה.

תאכלי תאכלי. במלחמה אנשים אפילו אכלו קליפות של תפוחי אדמה...

את צריכה להיזהר. לילה אחד כינים לקחו ילדה אחת מהמטה ליער...

את תמיד צריכה ללבוש תחתונים נקיים. אולי תמותי בתאונה ומה אז...

Ilana Zuckerman

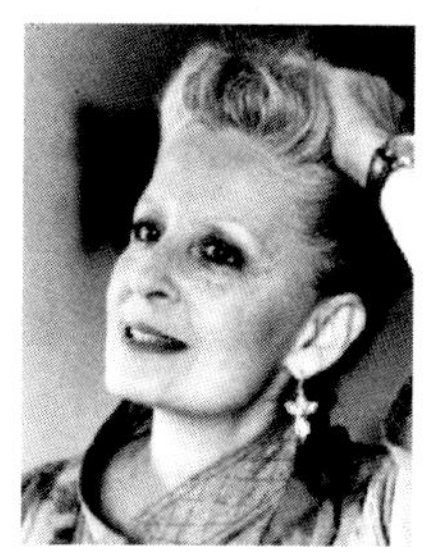

Lives and works in Jerusalem
In the 1980s, founded "Studio One" for radio art at the Israel Broadcasting Authority. Her works are widely broadcasted by dozens of radio stations in Israel, Europe, Canada, the U.S.A., and Australia.
Since 1990, has been active in the International Forum Ars Acoustica.

SELECTED WORKS

1996	*Artistic director, Israel Poetry Festival, "Poetry '96," Metulla*
	"Bird on Bird III," Music Festival, Kfar Blum, Israel
1995	*5 performances broadcasted live, International Poetry Festival, Jerusalem*
	"Bird on Bird" I and II, sound installation: "Sculpture in the Little Forest," Raanana, Israel, and Budapest, with Shuli Nachshon
	C.D. - Ars Acoustica.
	"White Nights," (Dostoevsky) soundtrack, Bama Theatre, Jerusalem
1994	*"Il Dolce Suono," Ars Acoustica, Macrophon Festival, Poland*
1993	*"Bird," sound installation Wings of Sound Festival, Finland*
	"The Angels of Tamara," Romaeuropa Festival
1992	*"Il Dolce Suono," Ars Sonora Festival, Spain, commissioned by Spanish State Radio*
1991	*"Primot," Macrophon Festival, Poland*
1990	*"Opus" collage, Audio-Box Festival, Italy*
1989	*"Bruno Schulz - a Portrait" collage, Futura Festival, Berlin*
1986	*"Anachronismus" collage, Audio-Box Festival, Italy*
1984	*"Elsa - an Homage", Prix Italia*
1982	*Composition for a woman's voice and jazz quartet, Tel Aviv Festival*

PRIZES

1994	*Ars Acoustica Prize for "Il Dolce Suono," Macrophon Festival, Poland*
1991	*First Prize for "Primot", Macrophon Festival, Poland*
1983	*Israel Radio Prize for "Elsa - an Homage"*

A point in memory begins to pulsate, expand, grow, and spread out, till it swallows everything. It leaves you expiring, imprisoned, in a web. Inward time, secret, freed from its tissue, burst and bled. It leaves behind confusion, destruction, sights and sounds in a blur. Echoes from other times reproduce themselves, are wrenched out of their place. Everything happens at once, runs amok, in a spiral which confuses all linear logic. A clash occurs between the hidden memory which bursts out, and the memory you are aware of and know well, and which deceives you. A clash between memory imprisoned in a recording machine on tape, the documentary material of memory which is supposed to be the objective sign, the proof, the map. But when the memory is taken out of the electronic system and deciphered, sensual and amorphous, it gives birth to unexpected significance, opens out, creates a new imaginary and fantastical environment. The sensuality and amorphousness of the sound create such strange contradictions, that make the sound so fully charged with significance.

The vital system of another life, another time, invades the present time of this life and leaves an imprint of paradoxical connections, echoes, doubts, dreams, touches of happiness and freedom. Freedom which is posible only when you have touched death again in the amputated time which you carry within yourself, as in pregnancy.

April 1996

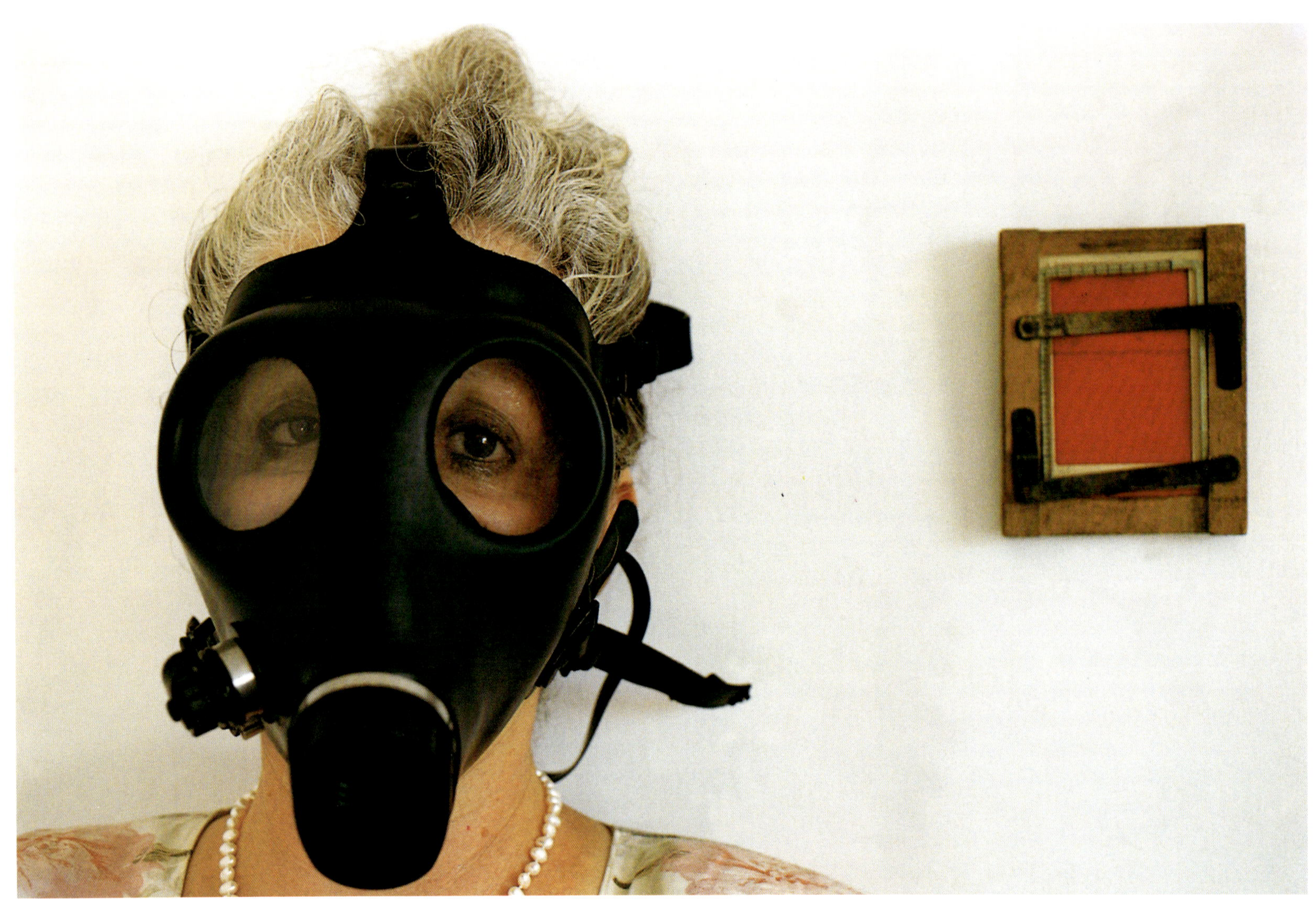

אילנה צוקרמן

נקודה בזכרון מתחילה לפעום, מתחילה להתרחב להתפשט עד שהיא בולעת. מותירה אותך מפרפר כלוא בתוך קורים. זמן פנימי, כמוס, השתחרר מרקמתו התפרץ ודמם. מותיר אחריו שבושים, הרס, מראות וקולות בערפל. הדים מתוך זמנים אחרים משכפלים את עצמם, חורגים ממקומם. הכל מתרחש בבת אחת, רץ בהול נשימה בתוך ספירלה הפורמת כל הגיון ליניארי.

מתרחש עימות בין הזכרון הכמוס המתפרץ לבין הזכרון הידוע לך, המוכר לך, לבין הזכרון הכלוא במכונת ההקלטה, בפס הקול, החומר התיעודי של הזכרון האמור להיות הסימון האובייקטיבי, ההוכחה, המפה. אבל כאשר הוא נשלף ומפוענח מן המערכת האלקטרונית – חושני, אמורפי, מוליד משמעויות בלתי צפויות, מפולש, הוא יוצר סביבה חדשה דמיונית עד להתמיה. החושניות של הסאונד והאמורפיות שלו יוצרים סתירה כה מוזרה ההופכת את הסאונד לטעון כל-כך.

מערכת חיונית של חיים אחרים – זמן אחר –פולשת אל תוך זמן חייך הנוכחי, משאירה אחריה חיבורים פרדוכסליים, הדים, ספקות, חלומות, נגיעות של אושר וחופש. חופש האפשרי רק לאחר שנגעת שוב במוות. בזמן הקטוע שאתה נושא בתוך כמו הריון.

אפריל 1996

Real Time in a Sealed Room,
1996
זמן אמיתי בחדר אטום

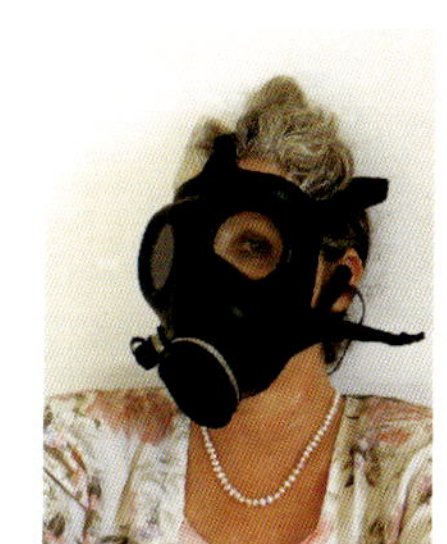
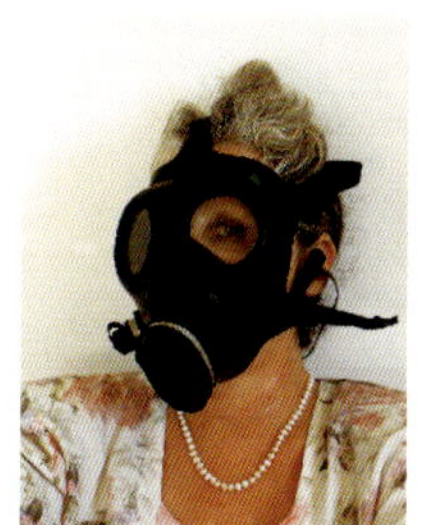
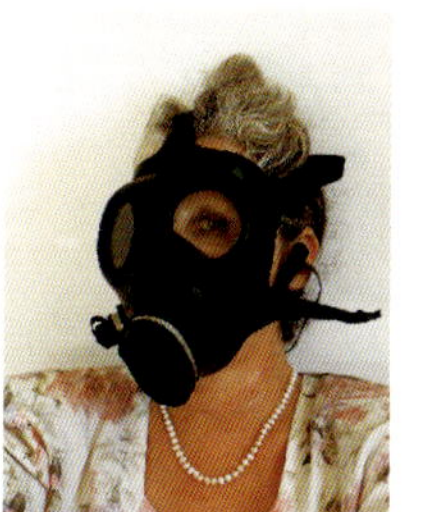
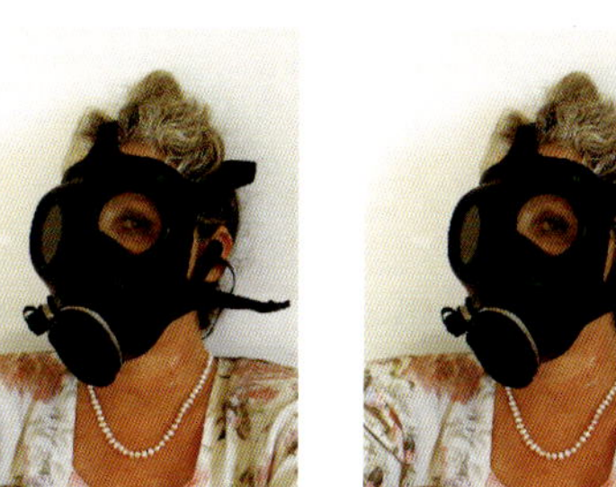
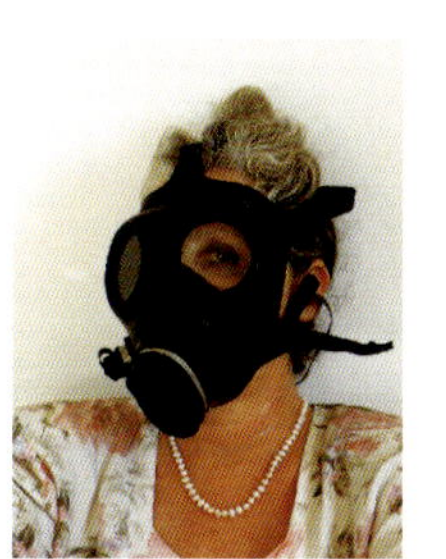
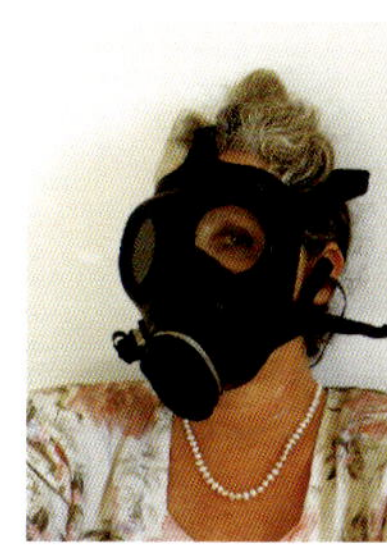

List of works

All works are lent by the artists unless otherwise specified. Measurements are in centimeters, height preceding width.

Elisha Dagan

Western 4 (Go . . D), 1992
Wood and industrial paint
170 x 100 x 580
Collection of Mishkan Leomanut, Museum of Art, Ein Harod

Ayana Friedman

Silent Environment, 1996
Installation, set of photographs on quilted fabric in a room
Fabric: 300 x 1200

Moshe Gershuni

Esther'l, 1994
Mixed media on canvas
116 x 89

Untitled, 1994
Mixed media on canvas
116 x 90
Untitled, 1995
Mixed media on canvas
100 x 100

Untitled, 1995
Mixed media on canvas
100 x 130

God Full of Mercy, 1996
Mixed media on canvas
60 x 60

Untitled, 1994
Mixed media on canvas
130 x 97

Untitled, 1994
Mixed media on canvas
130 x 97

The Sixth Day, 1988
Two cups, three dishes

Moshe Kupferman

Industrial Cardboard, 1995
Oils, graphite, and pencil on corrugated cardboard
106 x 106 x 12

Industrial Cardboard, 1995
Oils, graphite, and pencil on corrugated cardboard
106 x 106 x 12

Industrial Cardboard, 1995
Oils, graphite, and pencil on corrugated cardboard
106 x 106 x 12

Industrial Cardboard, 1995
Oils, graphite, and pencil on corrugated cardboard
106 x 106 x 12

Industrial Cardboard, 1995
Oils, graphite, and pencil on corrugated cardboard
106 x 106 x 12

Industrial Cardboard, 1995
Oils, graphite, and pencil on corrugated cardboard
106 x 106 x 12

Ariane Littman-Cohen

Virgin of Israel and Her Daughters, 1994
Installation, 20 beehives and red lights
Wood, wax, iron, electrical wire, red bulbs
30 x 41 x 56 each of 20

Daniel Sack

Untitled, 1992-93
Iron wire, ropes, plaster, pigment, epoxy-resin, aluminum shelf
Shelf: 37 x 2 x 25

Untitled, 1992-93
Iron wire, ropes, plaster, pigment, epoxy-resin, aluminum shelf
Shelf: 37 x 2 x 25

Untitled, 1994
Oil on wood
42 x 42

Untitled, 1993
Plaster, pigment, glass fibre, acrylic, epoxy-resin, strings
220 x 255 x 34

Untitled, 1992-93
Iron wire, ropes, plaster, pigment, epoxy-resin, aluminum shelf
Shelf: 37 x 2 x 25

Mani Salama

Untitled, 1996
Pencil, pastel, and graphite on old bookbinding
15 X 23

Untitled, 1996
Pencil, pastel, and graphite on old bookbinding
15 X 23
Untitled, 1996
Pencil, pastel, and graphite on old bookbinding
15,4 X 24

Untitled, 1996
Pencil, pastel, and graphite on old bookbinding
12,4 X 18,7

Untitled, 1996
Pencil, pastel, and graphite on old bookbinding
24 X 15,3

Untitled, 1996
Pencil, pastel, and graphite on old bookbinding
20 X 28

Untitled, 1996
Pencil, paste,l and graphite on old bookbinding
13,6 X 21

Untitled, 1996
Pencil, pastel, and graphite on old bookbinding
22 X 13,5

Untitled, 1996
Pencil, pastel, and graphite on old bookbinding
25,8 X 19

Untitled, 1996
Pencil, pastel, and graphite on old bookbinding
22,2 X 13,5

Untitled, 1996
Pencil, pastel, and graphite on old bookbinding
21,5 X 13,5

Micha Ullman

House, 1993
Pencil and gouache on paper
70 x 100

Day, 1990
Iron and red sand
17.8 x 32 x 24
Edition: 7/7

Havdala, 1990
Iron and red sand
17.8 x 32 x 27
Edition 7/7

Midnight, 1990
Iron and red sand
25.4 x 32 x 24
Edition 7/7

Signals, Signal 1, 1992
Sand print
50 x 70
Edition 50 AP

Signals, Signal 2, 1992
Sand print
50 x 70
Edition 50 AP

Signals, Signal 3, 1992
Sand print
50 x 70
Edition 50 AP

Signals, Signal 4, 1992
Sand print
50 x 70
Edition 30 AP

Yocheved (Juki) Weinfeld

History Series (I Milk), 1989-90
Mixed media
94 x 117
Collection of Doron Sebbag, O.R.S. Ltd., Tel Aviv

History Series (II Knife), 1989-90
Mixed media
96.5 x 117
Collection of Doron Sebbag, O.R.S. Ltd., Tel Aviv

History Series (III Razor), 1989-90
Mixed media
96.5 x 117

History Series (IV Ball), 1989-90
Mixed media
94 x 137

History Series (V Fish), 1989-90
Mixed media
63.5 x 132

Ilana Zuckerman

Real Time in a Sealed Room, 1996
Sound installation

(*) ״יום העצמאות״ של מדינת ישראל נבחר לתאריך הקמת המדינה, אך הוא אינו עצמאי בזמן, אלא חלק מרצף של שלושה ימים: יום השואה, יום הזכרון ויום העצמאות. הסידור הלינארי של שלושת הימים באופן כזה נקבע במתכוון, והוא יוצר מבנה נאראטיבי בעל אמירה סיפורית מתפתחת. הרצף שואה-גבורה-תקומה, מקביל לרצף היסטורי התפתחותי: העם שכמעט הוכחד, עמד על נפשו בגבורה, הדף את אויביו ובנה לעצמו מדינה משלו.

רצף סמיוטי זה הוא שהביא לכך שימי זכרון אלה התקבלו באופן טבעי בחברה בישראל, על אף הקושי הרב של היות יום הזכרון לחללי צה״ל נוגע ביום העצמאות תוך מעבר חד, אולי חד מדי.

עַם הַמְאַבֵּד אֶת זִכְרוֹנוֹ
מְאַבֵּד אֶת חַיָּיו.
עַם חַי מִמּוֹלֶדֶת וּמִקְבָרִים״

יורם קניוק
אלה אזכרה, על מות ועל מוות, אסופת שירים
עורכים: אריה בן־גוריון ובנימין יוגב, הוצאת הקיבוץ המאוחד, 1995, עמ׳ 124.

העבודות בתערוכה נעדרות פאתוס וסטריאוטיפ, וזאת משום שהתהוות הדימוי על בסיס הזכרון אינה בונה את הסיפור מחדש. כאן המשמעויות מטפטפות אל הדימוי מתוך ידע חיצוני לעבודה עצמה, והיא מהווה זרז לקריאת המשמעות הנסתרת. קריאת העבודה רב-משמעית: האם *הפסים* המכסים את עבודתו של משה קופפרמן קשורים לזכרונותיו כבנאי – מקצועו הראשון כעולה בקיבוץ – כאשר עסק בבניית שלדי עץ לבתים, או בעבודותיו כטפסן אז, או שמא הם עדות מעורפלת לפסי-רכבת או לגדרות התייל...

האם *החול האדום* בעבודותיו של מיכה אולמן הוא עדות למקום מגוריו – רמת השרון – שם האדמה היא אדמת-חול אדומה, או שמא זהו קשר לזכרון של אדמה ספוגת דמים...

הכוורות בעבודתה של אריאן ליטמן-כהן נראות גם כשדה-קברים, ואף אין להתעלם ממצלול המילים קבר/כוורת הנשמעים כזכר ונקבה; לכן, האם הדיון שלה בעולם המטריארכלי של הדבורים הוא הנושא המכסה על זכרון המוות?

כאן אנו רואים את עמעום הגבולות בין הזכרון האישי לבין הזכרון ההיסטורי הקולקטיבי, ומבינים שהאחרון עובר דרך מסננת הזכרון האישי; בעבודות האמנות שנוצרו, שחלקן שקטות וכמו נעימות לעין, יהיה קשה להבדיל בין זכרון של חרדה אפוקליפטית לזה של חרדה יום-יומית; בין סיוט הנובע מזכרון קולקטיבי לסיוט אישי פרטי; בין זכרון של דור שנכחד לזכרון של מות קרוב.

"הרצון היה לשכוח, להצפין עמוק את הזכרונות המרים בקרקעיתה של הנפש, מקום שעין זר, ואף לא שלך, לא תוכל להשיגם. כה חזק היה הרצון, עד אשר עלה בידינו לעשות את הבלתי־אפשרי. אין לדבר ואין לספר. זה היה הצו, והוא לא בא מבחוץ. מה לא עשינו כדי להעלים את הסוד האפל...

כאילו נולדנו כאן, על גבי הרים אלה, צמח מצמחי המקום...

מה לא עשינו כדי לעקור את כל שהיה עוד חבור אל אותו עולם ממנו באנו. בנינו לעצמנו מעין מושבת־עונשין פרטית, כדי שהיא, ברוב אלימות, תעקור כל זכר, כדי ששום תג לא יוכר בנו עוד..."

אהרון אפלפלד, **מסות בגוף ראשון,**
ירושלים תשל"ט, עמ' 36, 37, 38.

"...בתוך קולות התרועה, שגברו ונמשכו ביתר שאת, שהידהדו ממושכות עד למרגלות המרפסת, ככל שהרבו אלומות האור הססגוני להתנשא בשמים, – גמר רייה בלבו לרשום את סיפור המעשה המסתיים בזה, כדי שלא יהיה מאותם המחרישים, כדי להעיד לזכותם של מוכי־הדבר הללו, כדי להשאיר לפחות זכרון לעוול ולאלמוות שנגרמו להם, וכדי לומר, בפשטות, מה שלומדים בעיצומן של שואות, כי רבים בבני־האדם הדברים הראויים להערצה מאותם שיש לבוז להם.
אולם הוא ידע בכל זאת כי הרשומות הללו אין בהן להיות רשומות הנצחון האחרון. אין בהן אלא עדות למה שמוטל היה לעשותו, ואשר בלי ספק עוד מוטל לעשות נגד האימה וזרועה הנטויה, למרות קרעי־הנפש של כל האנשים אשר אם אין בכוחם להיות קדושים, הנה ממאנים הם לומר לנגף טוב, והם מתאמצים, על אף הכל, להושיט ידם לעזרה. ואכן בהאזינו אל קריאות השמחה העולות מן העיר, זכר רייה כי שמחה זו סכנה צפויה לה בכל עת. כי יודע היה מה שנעלם מן ההמון העלז הזה, ואשר ניתן הוא לקראו בכל הספרים, כי מתג הדבר אינו מת ואינו נעלם לעולם, כי יכול הוא לנוח, רדום במשך עשרות בשנים, ברהיטים ובכלי המיטה, כי מחכה הוא באורך־רוח בחדרים, במרתפים, במזוודות, בממחטות ובבלויי נייר, וכי, אולי יבוא יום, ולאסונם של בני־האדם וכדי ללמדם לקח, יעיר הדבר את עכברושיו וישלחם למות בעיר המתרוננת."

אלבר קאמי, ***הדבר,***

מצרפתית: יונתן רטוש, תל-אביב, 1968, עמ' 241־242.

"...שאלת הזכירה, על כל פנים, נשארת חשובה. עלינו לזכור לא רק את תאי הגזים אלא גם את המורכבות העשירה של החיים היהודיים באירופה שמתו בתוכם. הציונים מתעקשים שלא להחיות את זכרון החיים שנגדם התמרדו, אך זכירת השואה דורשת הערכה מחדש של הביקורת הציונית על העולם היהודי שנכחד. ובאשר לצורת הזכירה, הרי שהדרך היחידה הראויה להנצחת זכרון השואה היא באמצעות תיעוד מפורט ושליטה בעובדות. במקרה של השואה, ***השטן*** *מצוי בפרטים."*

אבישי מרגלית, "השימוש בשואה",
The New York Review of Books, *February 17, 1994.*

למראית עין אין חיי היום-יום נפגעים; אירועי תרבות מתקיימים, ספרות נכתבת, אמנות נוצרת, גנים נשתלים, קניונים נפתחים; אך בקפל שבלב רובץ העצב שהפך לחלק מהקיום של אלה ששכלו קרובים במשך השנים.

החברה הישראלית ממוקדת בילדיה, במסגרת המשפחה, בידידיה – ידידי נפש וחברים קרובים שהינם כמו בני משפחה לכל אחד ואחד מאתנו – ומושפעת עמוקות מכל אובדן. לכן השכול בארץ אינו רק אישי. קיימת הזדהות כלל-לאומית המתבטאת בימי זכרון והנצחה ובקיום קשרים הנמשכים לאורך זמן עם המשפחות השכולות.

כך הופכים תחושת הצער ועיבוד האבל קולקטיביים. (*)

באמצעות התערוכה ברצוני להתייחס לנושא הזכרון הקולקטיבי – של העבר הנשאר בתודעתנו, אמנם לא כפשוטו אלא בדימויו; דימויים אלה יכולים להשתנות על פי צורכי החברה, אם לבניית מיתוס, או בהתאם להשתקפות החברה בדימויים ובמיתולוגיה של עברה היא, או של חלקי עבר מתקופות או מתרבויות אחרות. החברה היא שבעצם יוצרת לעצמה עבר, דרך זכרון קולקטיבי שהוא היזכרות בעבר, עבר שאינו בהכרח דומה לעובדות ההיסטוריות. הבנת החברה את עברה הופכת מכשיר לקיום האמנות בהווה, על ערכיו שהשתנו.

דומה שאף הפרטים בחברה, ובמקרה שלנו – האמנים, שחלק ניכר מהם לא חווה אירוע אובדני באופן אישי, מעבדים את הטראומה, מנכסים אותה לעצמם או עורכים אותה באופן שתתאים לצורכיהם. התחושה הנוצרת אצל הצופה – כמו הטראומה שבה עוסקים האמנים – פרטית.

"... זו היתה השעה המיוחדת ההיא – אפילו עכשיו, אפילו כאן הכרתי אותה – שבמחנה אהבתי יותר מכולן, ואחז אותי רגש מכאיב וחסר־תכלית: של געגועים. בבת אחת הכל קם לתחייה, הכל היה כאן וגאה בי, כל הגוונים של מצבי־הרוח המוזרים שם הציפו אותי, כל הדברים הקטנים שעלו בזכרוני העבירו בי רעד.
כן במובן מסויים, החיים שם היו טהורים יותר, פשוטים יותר. נזכרתי בכל, ובזה אחר זה עלו בזכרוני כולם, גם אלה שלא עניינו אותי וגם אלה שרק ספירת המצאי הזאת והעובדה שאני כאן יכולות לשמש להם עדות: בנדי, ציטרום, פִּיטקה, בּוהוּש, הרופא וכל השאר... כבר התחלתי להרגיש איך גדלה ומתגבשת בי הנכונות: אני אמשיך לחיות את חיי שאי־אפשר להמשיך לחיות אותם... עוד לא נברא הדבר האבסורדי שלא נוכל לחיות אחריו, כמובן, וכבר עכשיו אני יודע שאי־שם בדרך אורב לי, כמו מין מלכודת שאי־אפשר לעקוף אותה – האושר. כי הרי אפילו שם, על־יד הארובות, היה ברווחי הזמן שבין הייסורים משהו שהיה דומה לאושר. תמיד שואלים רק על התלאות, על "הזוועות", בשבילי אולי דווקא זו תהיה החוויה שתיחרת לי בזכרון יותר מהכל. כן, על זה, על האושר של מחנות־הריכוז, אצטרף לספר להם בפעם הבאה, אם ישאלו.
אם ישאלו בכלל. ואם גם אני עצמי לא אשכח".

אימרה קרטס, ***ללא גורל****,*
מהונגרית: מרים אלגזי, תל אביב 1994, עמ' 194, 195.

הזהו אדם?

"אתם היושבים באין מחריד
במשכנות מבטחים;
אתם המוצאים מאכל חם ופני ידיד
בשובכם הביתה עם דמדומים:
התבוננו וראו הזהו אדם
העובד בביצה הקרה;
הוא, שאינו יודע מנוחה ונלחם
למען פת־לחם זעירה.
שבעבור "כן" או "לא" לבן־מוות היה.
התבוננו וראו האם אשה היא זאת.
בת בלי שם ובלא שיער;
שלא נותר בה עוד כוח לזכור,
שעיניה ריקות וצונן חיקה
כצפרדע ביום חורף וכפור.
הרהרו וזכרו כי כל זאת אירע.
והיו הדברים האלה:
אשר אנוכי מצווכם
לחקוק בלבבכם.
ושיננתם אותם לבניכם
בשבתכם בבית בלכתכם בדרך,
בשכבכם ובקומכם.
והיה כי תדומו – יאבדו בתיכם
ויך בכם החולי מכף רגל ועד קדקוד.
ויהפכו מכם פניהם יוצאי חלציכם, עוד."

פרימו לוי, ***הזהו אדם?****,*
מאיטלקית: יצחק גרטי, ירושלים 1988, עמ' 9.

מזעזעות במיוחד אינן נשכחות בנקל. טיבן שהן עולות מן הזכרון בתהליכים של היזכרות עם התבגרותו של האדם, לאחר שעברו תהליך של עיבוד.

בתערוכה זו ניתן ביטוי לא רק למועקת השואה אלא אף לקיום של חיים בצל סכנה ואיום מתמידים, על רקע זכרון של איום קודם בהכחדת העם היהודי כולו. אין בתערוכה דימויים ה"מייצגים" את "השואה", "הגבורה" ו"תקומת עם ישראל", אך ישנן יצירות אמנות שבהן השתיקה מאירה בצורה קוגניטיבית את תודעת העבר ותודעת ההווה, יצירות השולות מנבכי העבר את פירורי הזכרון ומגינות עלינו מפני טראומה נוספת, אם תבוא.

אני שנולדתי בארץ, מכירה – כמו כל ילידי הארץ – מציאות של חיים בצל סכנה ואיום תמידי על הקיום, במלחמה או בתקופות ארוכות של מתיחות אין-קץ ופיגועי חבלה. מציאות חיים זו הפכה נורמאטיבית, טבעית, לחיי שגרה; זאת כאשר קיימת השואה ברקע – בזכרון ההיסטורי הקולקטיבי של כל פרט בחברה; מכאן שנוצרים בארץ חיים, ולידם, כפי שאמר הסופר דויד גרוסמן, קיימת "הקלות הבלתי נסבלת של המוות – בגלל נוכחותם העזה מאד של המוות, סכנת המוות ופחד המוות, אפשר לחוש לפעמים בישראל בנטיה מעוותת לחוות את החיים כמוות לטנטי"; חיים המאפשרים להסביר את אופן ההתמודדות והקבלה, לכאורה, של הישראלי את המוות כחלק אינטגרלי מחייו.

הספר מגיע אל סיומו בזמן שהכל לא־ודאי. אמנם בפעם הראשונה מסתמנת אפשרות של שלום, אבל שום דבר לא בטוח. בפעם הראשונה, היציאה מן המנהרה נראית קרובה, אבל יש הרואים באור המנצנץ מרחוק תעתוע מסוכן... אבל – מעבר למחשבות על העתיד המיידי – אי הוודאות שבה אנחנו נתונים היא בעלת משמעות אחרת ומימד אחר. מאז ומעולם היא שאפיינה את ההוויה היהודית, ומבחינות רבות – לטוב ולרע – היא שעשתה אותנו למה שאנחנו. לפעמים, כשאני חושב על ההיסטוריה שלנו – לא זו של השנים האחרונות האלה, אלא על מהלכה כולו – מצטיירת לעיני איזו התרוצצות מתמדת, חתירה להשתרשות, לנורמליזציה ולביטחון, חתירה ששוב ושוב, דור אחרי דור, מועמדת בסימן שאלה; ואני אומר לעצמי שאולי גם המדינה היהודית היא רק שלב אחד בדרכו של עם, המסמל – בגורלו המיוחד במינו – את תהייתה הבלתי פוסקת, התהייה שתמיד מהססת ותמיד מתחדשת, של האנושות כולה".

*שאול פרידלנדר, **עם בוא הזכרון...***
מצרפתית: אליה גילדין, ירושלים 1980, עמ' 169־170.

"בני רץ אלי ואומר לי: בני.
אני אומר לאבי; שמע, בני, אני.
אבי רץ אלי ואומר לי: אבא,
שמעת? הוקם לנו זכר ושם.
אני רץ אלי ורואה: אני שוכב
כרגיל, פני אל הקיר, ורושם
בגיר על הקיר הלבן
את שמותיהם כולם, לבל אשכח
את שמי".

*דן פגיס, **"יוחסין"**,*
כל השירים, ירושלים 1991, עמ' 167.

"הזכרון, כידוע, ברבן ולעיתים אף חנפן. מסתמיות הימים וריקותם הוא מתבנת תבניות, בונה עלילות ואף נותן בהן משמעות."

"... היה עליו לאלף את זכרונותיו ולהדבירם כדי שיניחו לו לחיות, להרחיק מעליו את הכאב ואת האימה עד שייטשטשו וייעשו כחומר־גלם שעוד יילושו ממנו דברים אחרים.
כדי לברוח מאימי העבר היה עליו לטכסס טכסיסים, להסתתר, לטשטש את עקבותיו בעבר כדי שיוכל להמציא לו חיים אחרים".

"כך סיפר (דן פגיס) בפרקי "אבא" ובראיונות: "חשבתי שאצליח להימלט, ולא הצלחתי. כמו במחלות קשות שמתגלות רק לאחר זמן, אבל הן פורצות, כאן ארכה האינקובציה עשרים וכמה שנים (...) תמיד חשבתי שנושא השואה אינו ניתן לביטוי ספרותי – מפני שהמציאות ההיא חרגה מגבולות אנושיים. המציאות גברה על האותיות".

"אתה הוא כל הזכרונות שלך, קולך בוקע מהדי קולם".

*עדה פגיס, **לב פתאומי**,*
תל אביב 1995, עמ' 6, 84־85, 89, 117.

זכרון ארוך/ זכרון קצר

נלה קסוטו

רק בזכות השכחה
חיינו הם חיים
והם חיים בזכות הזכרון

ט׳ כרמי

הזכרון הינו הבנת העבר, בתהליך התבגרות שבו אנו משמרים חומרים מן העבר ומוסיפים להם אלמנטים המשנים את משמעותו; הבנתנו משתנה ובכך משתנה זכרוננו ואתו גם עברנו; לא העבר ההיסטורי העובדתי, אלא התייחסותנו הפרספקטיבית אליו.

לגבי, חלק ניכר מהזכרון קשור בכאב ובעצב אישיים, שהפכו עם הזמן לחלק מן הקיום היום-יומי. תהליך הברירה שמפעיל הזכרון הוא שאפשר את עיבודה מחדש של ממשות העבר וחשיפתם של היבטים ואפשרויות שלא עמדתי עליהם קודם. כך נתגבש אצלי הרצון לאצור תערוכה, שבה כל עבודת אמנות שאבחר להציג תהיה מושתתת על אותם יסודות המרעידים את נפשי: זכרון, כאב, עצב, שכחה ופחד המהולים יחד והם-הם היוצרים בעצם את עבודת האמנות.

עשרת האמנים המשתתפים בתערוכה זו מייצגים את העשייה האמנותית המתרחשת היום בישראל; בעבודותיהם טמון זכרון: של השואה, של המוות, של המלחמות.

״השפעת מועקת השואה קיימת אצל כל אמן ישראלי״ – כך אמר לי משה קופפרמן בינואר 1990, והוסיף, ״בגרו ובשלו אמנים החייבים לשאת את המועקה ולתת לה ביטוי״. דומני שאמירה זו של משה קופפרמן קשורה בפעולת הזכרון, או במילים אחרות, בכושרו הנפשי של היחיד להעלות ברגע מסוים את מה שאירע לו בעבר. ההיזכרות היא תהליך העלאתם של תנועות, מיומנויות, מוצגים, מילים, מושגים ועוד, ממה שנלמד בעבר; וחשובה לא פחות ממנה היא השכחה – שכמה סיבות לה, ובהן ההדחקה בלא יודעין מן התודעה אל הלא-מודע (״שכחה״) חוויות שאינן נעימות לנו; אולם חוויות

״שִׂים סֶכֶר גָּדוֹל
לְיַד מַעְיְנוֹת הַכְּאֵב
אֱגוֹר אִתּוֹ
כְּמוֹ מַיִם
שְׁמֹר עָלָיו
שֶׁלֹּא יִתְפַּזֵּר
כִּי הוּא חַיֶּיךָ.״

יונה וולק
אלה אזכרה, על מות ועל מוות, אסופת שירים
עורכים: אריה בן־גוריון ובנימין יוגב, הוצאת הקיבוץ המאוחד, 1995, עמ׳ 60.

...פעולתו של הדמיון קשורה לזכרון. הידעתם, הם יישרו את נהר המיסיסיפי בכמה מקומות, כדי לפנות מקום לבתים ולשטחי מחיה. מפעם לפעם מציף הנהר את המקומות האלה. ״מציף״, כך הם קוראים לזאת, אך למעשה אין זו הצפה; זו היזכרות. היזכרות במקומות שבהם נהג לזרום. למים זכרון מושלם והם מנסים תמיד לחזור למקום שבו נהגו לזרום. ואנו הסופרים דומים למים: זוכרים כמותם היכן היינו, באיזה עמק זרמה דרכנו, כיצד נראו הגדות, האור, והדרך המובילה למקום שממנו יצאנו. זהו זכרון רגשי – מה שזוכרים העצבים ומה שזוכר העור, לא פחות מחזות הדברים עצמה. ודחף של זכרון הוא–הוא ה״הצפה״ שלנו.
...ובכל זאת, כמו המים, אני זוכרת היכן הייתי לפני ש״יושרתי״.

טוני מוריסון, **״אתר הזכרון״**,
Out There, Marginalization and Contemporary Culture, The MIT Press, 1990, p.305

״האם יגיע לסף הכרתי הצלולה אותו זכרון, אותו רגע נושן, שחבלי קסם של רגע זהה לו באו ממרחקים לשדלו, לטלטלו, להרימו מקרקעית עצמי?
...ובבת אחת שב הזכרון ונגלה.
... משום שמזכרונות שנעזבו זמן כה רב מחוץ לזכרון, דבר לא שרד, הכל התפורר; הצורות –... – נמחקו, או, בהיותן רדומות, אבד להן כוח ההתפשטות שהיה מאפשר להן להבקיע אל התודעה. אבל, כאשר מעָבר רחוק דבר לא משתמר, במות האנשים, בהימוט הדוממים, הם לבדם, יותר שבריריים אבל יותר עזים, יותר על-חומריים, יותר עקשנים, יותר נאמנים, הם לבדם, הריח והטעם, נשארים עוד זמן רב, כמו נשמות, זוכרים, מחכים, מקווים, על תילי כל היתר, נושאים בלא רתע, על נטף אוורירי כמעט, את המבנה האדיר של הזכרון״.

מרסל פרוסט, **בעקבות הזמן האבוד**,
בצד של סוואן, חלק ראשון: קומברה, מצרפתית: הלית ישורון
הספריה החדשה, 1992, עמ׳ 50.

״... הסיפר הזה מתקרב לסיומו, ושוב נשאלת השאלה: האם הצלחתי לומר, ולו גם משהו, ממה שרציתי לבטא? למען האמת, התהייה הזאת, העימות הבלתי־פוסק הזה עם העבר במשך חודשים ארוכים, הפך כשלעצמו סיבה מספיקה ועניין הכרחי. ושוב עולות המילים של גוסטב מיירינק: ״עם בוא הידיעה, בא גם הזכרון, אט אט...״; אבל בסדר הפוך: ״עם בוא הזכרון, באה גם הידיעה, אט אט. ידיעה וזכרון דבר אחד הם...״

אוצרת: נלה קסוטו

ז כ ר ו ן   א ר ו ך | **זכרון קצר**

הגלריה העירונית לאמנות עכשווית, ראלי, צפון קרולינה

זכרון ארוך / זכרון קצר
עשרה אמנים ישראלים

22 באוגוסט - 9 בנובמבר, 1996

אוצרת התערוכה ועורכת הקטלוג: **נלה קסוטו**

עיצוב והפקת קטלוג: **סטודיו רמי וג׳קי / נגה**
תרגום ועריכה בעברית: **חנה שטרן**
צילום: **שי אדם**, עמ׳ 33, 35
עודד אנטמן, עמ׳ 31, 32
אברהם חי, עמ׳ 13, 14
סטפנו פונטבסו דה מרטינו, עמ׳ 12
ורנר זילין, עמ׳ 41
אלכס ליבק, עמ׳ 52, 53
מידד סוכובולסקי, עמ׳ 19, 21, 22, 23, 34, 36
יאיר פלג, עמ׳ 25, 27, 28, 29
נלה קסוטו, עמ׳ 1, 18, 24, 62
מהנדסי קול לעבודה
זמן אמיתי בחדר אטום: **זכי אגוזי**
מוטי ארנון

מספר קטלוגי 96-85944
ISBN 1-885449-03-8